Other Eagles In Leadership Books:

Reaching the World Series

Growing Missional Leaders

Gathering Missional Leaders

First Steps Discipleship

Intimacy With God Series

In His Image

In His Presence

Intimacy With God Resources

The Word In Worship Daily Devotional Journal

The Personal Prayer Journal

Living In Christ Series

Hope Enabler

Death's Shadow Valley Series

Entering Into Death's Shadow Valley

* You can find information about each of these books at
EaglesInLeadership.org

"Personal, warm and challenging to any facing loss and the journey of grief. Matthew gives us a personal glimpse of death, loss, grief and the impact it has on one's family, soul and faith. His reflective posture supplies for us, hope, health and opportunity to grow through loss! A worthy read for any. A companion for those who face loss and trying to live through it with grace and hope as new chapters of life opens"
~ Edward Hammett
Author of *Spiritual Leadership in a Secular Age*

Death is never easy. When it's a loved one it's so much harder. When it's your spouse, well. Doctor Matt Smith has entered, traveled through, and exited the Valley of the Shadow of Death. In this new book he shares his pain, sorrow, and the hope God gives to those who will but open their arms, trust God, and act on His mercy and grace.

This is a must read for anyone who is going through the trauma, has gone through the trauma, or is close to someone going through one of the most horrific pains of their lives … the death of their spouse. I recommend this book to all who grieve.
~ Wayne Elsey
CEO Funds2Orgs, Founder and former CEO Soles4Souls

This book written by Dr Mathew Lee Smith is very inspiring. It's an incredible book which explained how God can turn our grief into joy and equips us to swim through grief's tides. "Entering Death's Shadow Valley" gives people what they need when their lives turn dark. This book will satisfy you with God's awesome presence as it is an added opportunity to understand who God is and what he can do in spite of our situation.
~ Pastor T Ebenezer Sastry
President, Carmel Ministries
Eluru, India

This encouraging and prayerfully written book takes the reader through the phases of grief and loss. It brought to mind experiences and feelings from my own loss many years ago when I was encouraged and helped along by Dr. Matthew Lee Smith and his sweet wife, Melodee. Their Bible-based advice was to stay focused on God because He is with me always and to read the Bible daily and through in one year and look to the Lord for strength and guidance. You will find these same words of encouragement and much more in this book.
~ Sylvia Mathieu
Widow

This book will help and guide you in facing the darkest time of your life. It will teach and prepare you on how to overcome grief in a practical and spiritual way. It will make you appreciate and treasure your relationships - your spouse and the people you love. A great tool to build faith and hold on to God.
~ Pastor Tyrone I. Rovillos
Head Pastor of Citylight Church
Taguig City, Metro Manila
Philippines

Entering Into
Death's Shadow Valley

(Experiencing the Reality that they are Gone Forever)

Dr. Matthew Lee Smith, Ph D

EIL Publishing
A Division of Eagles In Leadership

Los Angeles, California, USA

Kiwatule, Kampala, Uganda

EaglesInLeadership.org

Entering Into Death's Shadow Valley: *Experiencing The Reality That They Are Gone Forever*

Published by EIL Publishing
2020 Los Angeles, California, USA
Kiwatule, Kampala, Uganda

For more information about Dr. Matthew Lee Smith, please visit his website at EaglesInLeadership.org

Table of Contents

Dedication

I dedicate this book, *Entering Into Death's Shadow Valley,* to you. Your journey wasn't chosen, it was forced upon you. And yet, because you have picked this book up, you have shown that indomitable spirit that conquers the hardest of things in life.

While you might not feel very brave or courageous right now, I want to assure you that you are far more able to do this than you might imagine! Great things are about to happen in your life. God will show up and show off! So, to you! I dedicate this book to your success while *Entering Into Death's Shadow Valley!*

I also want to dedicate this book the one person who birthed the idea, my Pastor's wife, Marisa Sarile. It was her idea to write this book and her encouragements to keep at it when things got too emotional or frustrating. Thank you, Marisa, for the long hours of discussion in those first months especially. I would not have been able to sort out all the pain and sorrow, the hope and light without you listening and giving wise advice. Here it is! Even thought I was not in favor of the idea at the beginning. Thank you for encouraging me to write this!

Preface

Entering Into Death's Shadow Valley is my journey through the horrific process of losing my life-partner, Melodee Joy. It is meant to help others who enter this treacherous and often perilous path understand that it is ok to grieve, but it is not ok to camp or live in that deadly valley!

Grief, as I will often say within the pages of this book, is a monster that seeks to destroy us if we refuse to embrace our faith relationship with King Jesus, lean heavily on the strength of the Holy Spirit, and depend on the wisdom of the words of God from our Bibles as our daily nourishment.

If you are grieving, you have my deepest empathy and sympathy. This is a journey no one wants to embark upon. And every one of us has a *different* path to take when we are *Entering Into Death's Shadow Valley.* However, we also have many things in common ... experiences, obstacles, and dangers.

Perhaps my story will help you, or someone you know. It's written from a reluctant heart. I did not want to write this book. I did not enjoy writing this book — as I had to relive every emotion as I typed these words. However, I was compelled from the start to write this book ... and maybe another one or two.

In any event, I want you to know that this is a transparent journey I am taking you on. It is emotional as well. One of my friends said, *"Wow, I just read, "My Story," and "the Grief Announces Itself." How you tell the story is like I was part of the story. It feels like I was there because while reading, the questions in my mind were, "How, When, Why?" And so far you answered it."*

If this record of my painful journey will help you, then I will deem this project a success. Of course, I would love to hear from you! Feel free to message me at: http://eaglesinleadership.org/contact.

You have my sincere gratitude for picking this book up. And you have my deep admiration for standing strong in the midst of this!

Introduction

Grief. King David of Israel long ago was correct when, in Psalm 23:4 he called it, *"The Darkest Valley,"* (NIV), (CSB), (CEB), (HCSB), (NLT), or *"The Valley of the Shadow of Death,"* (ESV), (MEV), (NKJV).

If you are personally, intimately acquainted with this horrific messenger of death, then I want to tell you I understand and I am sorry. Your pain is overwhelming. Your ache is unbearable. Your relief seems impossible. You are hemorrhaging from every emotional and psychological orifice possible … many of which you weren't ever aware of. And all you want is for it to stop. For things to return to normal. For your loved one back.

And that, my dear friend, is the problem. While our minds know that isn't possible, our hearts wish it to be so … overwhelmingly, uncontrollably, totally so. And so we bleed. Most of us do it in silence, behind closed doors. We stay away from people because we don't have the energy to keep it together, much less be with people who want to shower us with platitudes and clichés – no matter how well meaning they may be. We simply cannot take it!

And so we sit, often in darkness. Most often in silence or, if we can't stand our thoughts, we turn on the TV hoping the drone of endless, unintelligible babble – *We aren't really listening, are we?* – will drown out the voices in our heart, the whispers of our heart and the darkness of our soul.

This book is a journal of sorts, a transparent record of the despair of losing the love of my life, my symbiotic life partner, and the journey I was forced to endure in those opening days, weeks and months. But I was not alone. Because of my strong faith and intimate relationship with King Jesus, I was equipped to handle some of this onslaught more effectively because I simply know and have followed the same truth that King Jehoshaphat of Judah, (Southern Kingdom, Israel), did so long ago when invaded by the joint forces of the Moabite and Ammonite Armed Forces...

"Our God, will you not judge them? For we have no power to face this vast army that is attacking us. We do not know what to do, but our eyes are on you."" (2 Chronicles 20:12, NIV)

As the book title relates, there are *five realities* we must face right now. When we do, with God's help and our eyes on Him, I am here to tell you that you will be able to one day – maybe not right away – but one day experience the hope and joy David describes both inside and once we depart *Death's Shadow Valley:*

"Even though I walk through the darkest valley, I will fear no evil, for you are with me; your rod and your staff, they comfort me. You prepare a table before me in the presence of my enemies. You anoint my head with oil; my cup overflows. Surely your goodness and love will follow me all the days of my life, and I will dwell in the house of the LORD forever."
(Psalm 23:4–6, NIV)

REALITY #1: ENTERING

Unfortunately, this is *just the beginning.* It won't get easier for a while. Things are going to be messy, ugly, painful, dark, suffocating, and awful – much of the time all at once. We enter this dark valley unwanted. It wasn't your choice. Every shred of your being wishes it wasn't so, but it is. Now we have to, somehow, deal with the horrible reality. *That's why I wrote about my journey.* I want to provide some light in the midst of your darkness, so that your steps may be a bit more sure as you stumble through your days.

REALITY #2: INTO

Immersion is the only way to describe this, unless you prefer the result of immersion: *drowning.* Both are apt. We have been thrown *into* this. Whether by accident, disease, age, enemy, or events ... we are in it up to our eyeballs and we can't avoid that reality as much as we seek to deny it, to decry it, or to delay the reality of it.

This is simply one place we *never* wanted to be! And while we are *in it* we yell with all our might, *"We don't want to be here! We were forced to be here!"* But, as much as we shout and scream, nothing changes. *Venting doesn't lead to better … but it sure will make us bitter!*

Just as when my mother threw me into the deep water and told me to swim – an incredibly crazy tactic I admit – so, too, was the way I felt at Melodee's death. I had to make up my mind to *swim* despite not knowing how, just as I did so long ago in the waters that wanted to suffocate me! Today I am here to tell you to *swim!* Even if you don't know *how – just swim!*

Keep your head afloat! Read on in this book. Let me share some helps. Let me tell you the truth – often brutal, visceral – but always honest. We can't get out of the deep when we choose to ignore the danger! So, choose to splash ahead! Page by page you will find help, hope, and some healing from the hurt.

REALITY #3: DEATH

Ok. I said it. *Death.* We are fighting for *our lives* because the one whom we loved so much *has died.* Death – on this side of eternity – is so permanent. It changes everything. The more I walked through the fog and the darkness of that valley, the more I realized that *she wasn't coming back!* Nothing I could do would change that. Nothing I could pray would turn things around. *Nothing would bring Melodee back!*

While we all have heard the trite sayings, *"Every birth is the announcement of a death,"* we surely don't consciously think that applies to *our loved ones* – at least not *now!* And when the cold, brutal reality sets in, it numbs the soul, turns the mind to sludge, and shatters the heart in ways no one can seem to put back together.

Ugly. Unfair. Unrelenting. Death has a way of demoralizing the soul and the spirit so that all we want to do is crawl up in the darkness and die ourselves. *And THAT is what this book is all about.* While *"the thief's purpose is to steal and kill and destroy,"* I am here to testify that Jesus' *"purpose is to give [you] a rich and satisfying life."* (John 10:10, NLT)

It may not seem possible, or even probable right now. Amidst the gloom and doom you can't see any way out of this. However, being years down the road now, I am here to tell you, Jesus' words here are so very true. I have tested them and found them to be 100% accurate. In ways I cannot even understand, God has not only brought me out of *Death's Shadow Valley,* He has also given me *"a rich and satisfying life."* (John 10:10, NLT)

REALITY #4: SHADOW

For those of us who are truly disciples (committed followers) of Jesus of Nazareth, the King of kings and Lord of lords, the Giver of Life – abundant and eternal life – *death is just a shadow.* Remember so clearly what the Bible teaches us, *"During the forty days after He suffered and died, He **appeared** to the apostles from time to time, and He **proved** to them in many ways that **He was actually alive**. And He talked to them about the Kingdom of God."* (Acts 1:3, NLT)

Once Jesus was finished giving His final instructions to His disciples, *"He was **taken up** into a cloud while they were watching, and they could no longer see Him."* (Acts 1:9, NLT) Now, we know, that *"But in fact, Christ has been **raised from the dead**. He is the first of a great harvest of all who have died. So you see, just as death came into the world through a man, now **the resurrection from the dead** has begun through another man. Just as **everyone dies** because we all belong to Adam, **everyone who belongs to Christ will be given new life.** But there is an order to this resurrection: Christ was raised as the first of the harvest; **then all who belong to Christ will be raised when he comes back.**"* (1 Corinthians 15:20–23, NLT)

And lest we are heart broken about these words, let us remember, *"Yes, we are fully confident, and we would rather be away from these earthly bodies, **for then we will be at home with the Lord**."* (2 Corinthians 5:8, NLT) Therefore, we have a clear reality that when we know and love King Jesus as the Rescuer of our Soul and as Our Life (Colossians 3:4), we can be assured that our earthly death is simply a moment of transition to our New Life in Heaven with our King and Lord!

Thus, death is a shadow … one that shifts and turns and disappears with time as we realize that it may be dark here on Earth right now, but the hope we have that we will one day be reunited with them, to enjoy them *forever* in a place that is **real, solid, and dependable** and pales in comparison to our wildest imaginations. Light for our darkness. Pushing back the darkness of our despair. Penetrating the gloom of our grief. Pouring into our souls the hope of Heaven … all reminding us that while yes, it is so painful now, THIS is what our faith is all about … *overcoming the physical limitations of this life = death.*

God has given us abundant and **eternal** life. So, death is but a painful shadow for this season. Soon, we will be on "the other side" and *"He will wipe every tear from their eyes, and there will be no more death or sorrow or crying or pain. All these things are gone forever."* (Revelation 21:4, NLT)

REALITY #5: VALLEY

You are *trapped* right now! You might not even realize it, though I am pretty sure most of us do. The reality is that feeling miserable can become a comfortable way of life. *After all, if it wasn't, why are SO many people living in that grief-infused misery?*

This is a valley, between two mountain ranges. One was your life before the death of your loved one. The other is your life after this valley. You are just entering this valley and it may seem big, dark, dangerous, and deadly. *It is!* Many come in but *never walk out!* I see them every week.

Their loved one died five, ten, 20 years ago and they are *still in the valley, still trapped in the pain, still nursing the hurt, still struggling with their feelings and emotions.* Trapped. *By their own choice.* They got comfortable with the pain and refused to do the hard things, to make the hard choices, to move forward into all that God NOW has for them. And so, they sit. They sulk. They sour.

People don't come by often. They *can't.* Those people are simply too gloomy and despairing to be with. They entered into *Death's Shadow Valley.* The journey became difficult. They decided to camp by the streams of sorrow. The built a small shelter. As time passed, they became accustomed to their sorrow and misery and simply decided to live there *until they die!*

Death's Shadow Valley is a trap. It is an arduous trek through the badlands. However, we were not meant to live in this Valley! We are to travel *through* it. Then we are to exit it so we can enjoy all that God has for us!

And where are we going? To a banquet! *Despite* our grief, God wants to bring life and that more abundantly to us! Listen to David one more time: *"You **prepare a feast for me** in the presence of my enemies. You **honor me** by anointing my head with oil. My cup **overflows with blessings.** Surely **your goodness and unfailing love will pursue me** all the days of my life, and I will **live in the house of the Lord** forever."* (Psalm 23:5–6, NLT)

God has a great plan for you! He needs **you** to choose life, not the horrible, debilitating doom of being alive while trapped in *Death's Shadow Valley.* That's why I wrote this book – as painful as this process has been for me. I wanted to help you move *out of the Valley!* I wanted to show you that the things you are experiencing are *normal* in this season. It's ok to be sad and cry a lot. It's ok to feel lost and without hope. However, this too will pass *if we make the effort* to walk with our King and trust Him enough to do what He says, believing He has more for us to do before we stand on Heaven's shore with our loved one.

God has a plan for the rest of your life. This book seeks to help you get up and get moving so you can enjoy the rest of your life in the abundance He has planned for you!

Follow me. I came back to get you! You've stayed here long enough. Turn the page and let's get going!

My Story

Melodee's Endometrial Cancer Returned

"Even though I walk through the valley of the shadow of death,
I will fear no evil, for you are with me."
(Psalm 23:4)

"I'm sorry, Melodee. There's no easy way to say this. I've run out of tricks in my bag. We can't stop this." Those words from Dr. Lynda Roman of Keck Hospital of USC in Los Angeles are seared into my soul – branded as with a hot iron.

All of our fighting over the past seven and a half months had come to this. The prayers, fastings, pleadings, cryings, all came down to this... and it felt like defeat.

How could I let go of the light of my life, my "Ivory Beauty?" As I tell people to this day, "We weren't just *married*. We weren't *happily* married. We were a symbiosis." As Tabitha, our oldest daughter said at Melodee's memorial, our love for one another would make people gag!

And now, with that one conversation, the end was in sight and my heart was breaking. As we held each other after the door closed and cried our eyes out, there was still so much we wanted to say, wanted to do – in fact, we were scheduled to leave for Israel in just 4 weeks to lead a tour group!

Now, all those plans, all those hopes and dreams were gone. What we had hoped would be decades now came down to days... about 11 to be exact.

Shattered but Surrendered

As Melodee lay there in her hospital bed, and I sought to remain strong in my faith – though *this* would test it to its limits – the tears simply wouldn't stop flowing. Melodee would soon enjoy a painless life in Heaven. Her faith in Jesus was unshakable... to the very end.

In the quiet though, I realized I would soon be all alone. *Of course, I would have the grace of the Lord Jesus and the mercy of God to support me.* But, there, in the quiet of her room at Keck Hospital of USC I realized it would soon just be Jesus and me.

She insisted I go home that night and get some sleep – she knew I couldn't rest on the fold out chair "bed" in her room. Sleep?! How?! As I knelt beside my bed at home that night, that bed where for months I had pled for Melodee's total and complete healing, with tears flowing I simply cried out to Jesus a brand new prayer… a deeper prayer of faith: *Lord, this plan sucks… but I am surrendered! Not my will, but Yours' be done. All I have EVER wanted Lord is Your will: Nothing more, nothing less, nothing else."*

Only Seven Months?

Could it have only been seven months earlier that Melodee's side pain was so great we went to the ER while visiting our youngest daughter, Hannah, and her family in Oklahoma? Thinking it was kidney stones, we waited for the test results on March 28, 2017 only to be told her endometrial cancer had returned.

What had started as a trip to help our daughter's family prepare for a move became six weeks of doctor's appointments, biopsies, strategizing and, ultimately, a trip to MD Anderson in Houston.

How Melodee made that trip to Houston still astounds me. Unknown to us she was in the first evidences of severe osteoporosis. She had a hairline crack in one of her vertebrae and was in excruciating pain. Strong pain meds and an iron will to get to Houston well afforded her the stamina to make the trip.

At MD Anderson the doctor's confirmed the diagnosis and set a treatment regimen. Suggesting that the process would be longer and that it might be easier to receive the treatment at USC in Los Angeles where we had a large support group and after a hospitalization for pain related complications, we finally boarded a plane for her last trip home to Los Angeles.

Unfortunately, we were homeless at the time. I had lost my fulltime pastor position and we were in transition. Our possessions were packed in storage and our home had just sold. Melodee's sister invited us to stay at their home while we got situated. So, when we returned to LA we decided to stay in a hotel that first night to make the trek to her sister's home, some 90 miles east, easier.

As we went to the room, the elevator door hit her in the back. Pain shot through her. Unknown to us at the time, she had cracked three vertebrae. She went to the hospital via ambulance after a day of agony.

With little accomplished after four days in the hospital, she was released on Father's Day. After two weeks of recovery Melodee was again in pain and, on the fourth of July, she was back in the ER.

With numbness creeping up her leg, we contacted our USC doctors and they wanted her to be transferred, which we did. The back pain was so intense that at one point she said, "I just want to die!" That was the ONLY time I heard her complain about her pain – and that wasn't the cancer, it was the osteoporosis!

On July 18, after ten days in the hospital, two back surgeries, and chemo Melodee was ready to be released… but to where? We could no longer stay at her sister's house and we had nowhere else to go. So, we put out the word to our support group via Facebook and through our prayer partners.

To our blessing and amazement, Pastor Bryan, Marisa and Micah Sarile who live just five miles from the hospital welcomed us into their home with all the inconvenience that would entail. Giving up Pastor's prize room and a bathroom, they did everything they could to make us comfortable and welcome.

Recovery Thwarted

Weekly trips to and from USC, sometimes two or three times a week, became routine. Melodee's recovery was going well. Her back hurt less each week, she was walking well and we were looking forward to our trip to Israel the week after Thanksgiving.

Friends donated to help her get a walker and other needed items while Pastor Bryan, Marisa, and Micah waited on us hand and foot. Laughter filled the house as these people of great grace told us repeatedly, "You're family!"

As Melodee's osteoporosis got better, so did her cancer treatment. Finally, after the fourth round on October 17, Dr. Roman gave Melodee the choice of more chemo or a pill that would hold the tumors in check. This treatment would be something she would be able to take for decades and keep the cancer in stasis. She opted for the latter.

Quickly Melodee developed stomach issues and after an admission to the hospital on October 27 it was discovered that the cancer had mutated and exploded into overdrive.

Last Days, Last Conversations

Fifteen days after Melodee's admission to Keck Hospital of USC in Los Angeles she stood on Heaven's shore, welcomed by her Lord and Savior whom she loved and had served for most all of her life.

As I walked into her room the morning after Dr. Roman's fatal news, my wife had taken on a different attitude, a different spirit. She was ready for the transition. While I was still working through the agony, it was like she had embraced the reality and was willing to accept all that God had planned.

She began preparing *me* for the journey ahead. She gave instructions, orders, and directions throughout the days. She planned her memorial in almost every detail, explained the finances and the locations to all her passwords and files on her computer and in the file box. One day, after one final test, she was groggy and we were talking about finances. I was explaining some numbers and – although in a semi-conscious state – she quickly gave me the total! *Melodee was always the book keeper on this journey and not even some strong drugs were going to impede her ability to help me get the numbers right.*

Most amazing were the conversations that dealt with me. Each day she gave me directions, advice, counsel, as she organized her final wishes which included the non-optional directive: "You. Will. Get. Married. Again. Wait one year!"

As friends came and went, she so appreciated their love and care and engaged each one as much as she was. Melodee arrived home around 4 pm on Friday evening, November 10, to hospice care. While the trip wasn't fun, she was glad to be back home.

Final Hours

They say that one's true character is shown as they face the end of their life on earth. That was never truer than with my Melodee Joy.

Around 7 p.m., dear friends Pastor Willie and Josie Sangalang came to visit along with their daughter, JoJo. Melodee was only eight hours from promotion to Heaven, yet she was alert and fully engaged. As Pastor's family was leaving, Melodee started saying, "Thank you!" which she repeated for several minutes after they had left. *Melodee's gratitude is a trademark I will cherish for eternity.*

As we talked she kept saying, *"You have been and always will be my best friend."* Repeating those words over and over and over for several minutes, *Melodee showed me her deep love and loyal friendship to the very end and that was the basis of our partnership in this life.*

A little later, after having been quiet for a while, she said, "I want to go to Heaven first." I responded, "Well, I think you're going to get your wish." She got quiet for a few minutes and I went to take care of something else. Then, all of a sudden, she said, "Ha! Ha! Ha!" Since it had been a while since we had spoken, at first I didn't get it. As she kept saying, "Ha! Ha! Ha!" it finally it dawned on me and I asked, "Are you laughing at me because you get to go first?" And she said, "Yep! Ha! Ha! Ha!" *Melodee's absolute confidence in the assurance of eternal life with the Lord who died in her place for the atonement of her sins was so strong that she found it funny she got to go before me.*

A while later she asked me, "Would you play some of *your* music?" *"My* music?" I asked. "Yes!" she said. So, I went to my *Spotify* playlist and started playing the group *Elevation* – a contemporary Christian worship group. As the words played praise to our Amazing God, Melodee started saying loudly, "Yes Lord! Thank you! Praise Your name!" *As I listened to her praise God, I realized she was preparing herself for her imminent arrival. Her lifelong passion was coming to fruition and she was ready to step on Heaven's shore.*

The wee hours of the morning began to show us she wasn't long for this world when she asked, "What's that guy doing here?" We looked out the door where she indicated seeing him and Jamie, the hospice nurse asked, "Is he scary?" She said, "No." Then both the nurse and I asked, "What's he doing?" She responded, "Nothing. He's just hanging around." *It was at that point I knew that an angel was stationed outside of our bedroom keeping watch to escort this mighty warrior of the faith – my wife – home to her eternal reward.*

It wasn't long after that Melodee breathed her last, and all I could think about was the song her mother, Shirley, used to sing:

But just think of stepping on shore - And finding it Heaven!
Of touching a hand - And finding it God's!
Of breathing new air - And finding it celestial!
Of waking up in glory - And finding it... home!

The Road Ahead

To say the days and weeks after her departure have been difficult is an understatement. Hours of tears and heartbreak followed. However, in the midst of this journey of grief, I have learned and keep learning so much.

Without the heart and compassion of a few key people, I doubt I would be where I am today on this side of healing and health. I have found them to be wise and honest, transparent and trustworthy – all that everyone who walks through the Valley of the Shadow of Death needs.

As I share what I have learned, I hope and pray that God will help you move forward; to heal, to reclaim the amazing and abundant life God wants for each and every one of us.

And I must say, this is a book I did *not* want to write. Without my host family I wouldn't be healing as quickly as I am. Each one pours the oil of gladness into my soul on a daily basis. One day, Marisa said, "Pastor Matt, you need to write a book on grief… while you're going through it." I quickly dismissed her suggestion. Then, I found myself arguing with God for a couple of weeks.

On an onramp to the 110 southbound freeway one afternoon, God said, "These are some of the topics I want you to cover in the grief book!" Then, about twenty chapter ideas came flowing so quickly I could hardly write them down fast enough! (We won't talk about the moving violation I committed.)

When I arrived home I showed the list to Pastor, Marisa, and Micah and said, "I guess I'm writing a book on grief!"

The thoughts and ideas here are meant to bring hope and to heal, to move you forward in faith and life. Thank you for picking this book up. I pray that as God heals your broken heart some of our words will help.

1

Grief Announces Itself

Experiencing Your Soul Mate's Departure

"It is appointed for man to die."
(Hebrews 9:27)

He was young and obviously shaken. The doctor was weeping! We thought he would come in and tell us that the Melodee has some kidney stones and she might have to have them removed through a process called lithotripsy. This is a process where the doctor using ultrasound shock waves to break up the stones into small pieces so they can be passed by the body. *Nothing* could have been farther from the truth!

It had all started so innocently. We were just starting to pack our youngest daughter, Hannah, and our son-in-love, Michael's home for their imminent move. Melodee is a master at packing and so things were getting started well. Then, she started to complain of side pain. Since she never wanted to go to the hospital, I joked with her, *"Do you want me to take you to the hospital?"* To my surprise she said, *"Yes."*

So after the short drive, Hannah dropped us off and went back to take care of her young children. The tests came and then we waited… wondering what would happen next. There was so much packing yet to do and she was eager to get to it, but the pain.

When the doctor explained the seriousness of the situation – several large tumors – and that we could consult their oncologist, we knew things were grave. As he wept, and as we sat there in shock, life seemed to blur. In the quiet of that exam room, we looked into each other's eyes knowing that everything had just shifted… seriously. As tears came, we prayed for God's presence and healing.

Blindsided and Numb

To say that our emotions went wild would be to undersell the reality. On the long, quiet ride back to Hannah and Michael's home it seemed like every scenario possible was conceived and experienced. Our hearts were ripped out.

We bled emotionally all over the back seat of the van on the dark drive back from the hospital.

Shock numbs. To be perfectly honest, much of what happened those next few days is lost in the fog of shock. Like a murky night in London, shock seems to surround and obscure everything familiar and certain. Its cold tentacles wrap themselves around our minds and blinds us to everything except shock's traveling companion... fear.

Fear paralyzes. Icy with its touch, fear seems to freeze the soul in ways that are virtually inexpressible. If you are reading these words as a fellow traveler in pain, then you know the grip fear has. Strong. Ruthless. Paralyzing.

Our senses seem to shut off... or run wild, depending on how God has built us. For me, who usually has dozens of thought-streams flowing through my mind at any given moment, all I could do was feel fear: Fear of loss, fear of the process, (My mother and father both died of cancer), and fear of being alone. Fear. Cold. Icy. Fear.

Love bleeds. And yet, at the same moment, I was bleeding for the Love of my Life. How could this happen? She lived such a right life. Don't get me wrong. Melodee wasn't sinless. But, she lived a much purer life than most of the people I have ever met. She loved God on a first name basis. He answered *her* prayers before He would answer mine! *(And I was a pastor all my adult life!)*

There was so much left for her. We were young. Just stepping into a new season and we were certain it was for better things. While we didn't know what our future held, we were certain we knew that God has a good plan for us. (Jeremiah 29:11)

Now, as I looked into the eyes of my Beloved, I saw her sorrow and fear. Her mother had died from cancer also. It was Melodee who stayed with Mom every day of the week, Monday through Friday, while Dad worked. She tended and cared, cleaned and covered her in prayer. Now, I could see in her eyes the love for me. Her passion *not to have me* go through what she had done for her mom.

Uncertainty reigns. But nothing in life is certain except that one day we will all die. As much as I wanted to put that fact into some little box and hide it away from the life we were enjoying as we served our Lord and Savior, here it simply announced itself and did so with the force of a baseball bat over our heads.

What would happen next? Would she want treatment? I remember her saying more than once that she never wanted chemo. Would she be healed? We serve a miracle-working God who raises the dead and heals the sick. In fact, *"by faith we understand that the universe has been created <u>by a word from God</u> so that the visible came into existence from the invisible."* (Hebrews 11:3, CEB) All we needed was *"a word from God"* and Melodee would be whole again!

Faith Struggles. Back home in the room we'd taken over from our two oldest granddaughters, Isabella and Heidi, we wept and prayed for a miracle from this God we had served *all our lives since salvation!* We pled the blood of Jesus. We called on God's mercy and compassion. We were fervent in prayer.

Yet, with all our experiences with God, and all the scripture we had memorized and internalized, I found myself struggling. At times I thought this was some grand test that God had brought to us so He could *show up and show off*, for His glory in our story. At other times, when the darkness of the night hours overtook and I heard my Love sleeping, I wept and cried out to God in agony not wanting to lose her.

Cancer was no friend to our lives and, here again; it had popped its ugly, horrific, menacing head up and laughed at our faith. Seeking to destroy who we are and pry us from our certainty in the One who had *"loved you with an everlasting love,"* we continued to hold Him to the promise of His own words, *"therefore I have continued my faithfulness to you."* (Jeremiah 31:3) How we needed His continued faithfulness now more than ever!

Unwanted Visitor

When death announces itself, it reveals who *we really are*. Not the social media version. Not the one our family and friends think we are. Surely not the Church House one. No, when death comes calling, everything we are is on display for all to see. How we handle such an unwanted visitor sets a path that eventually will bring health and healing or depression and darkness.

Be honest! The worst strategy is to ignore what is happening. Death is knocking. Whether we liked it or not we had to acknowledge it. We needed to talk things through. We were a couple. We went through *everything together.* Attacks from so-called Christian leaders, times of financial shortage, sickness, the death of our parents, and so many other things had found us standing back to back facing every one of these difficulties together. We would go through this – our worst difficulty so far – *together* as well.

That required being honest. Sharing our fears, our uncertainties, our frustration, our sadness, was all part of it. We also knew we both needed time to process what we were thinking and feeling. So, that would take some times alone and quiet as well.

Looking back, I'm so grateful to Pastor Russell Gabler who in 1992 had encouraged me in reading God's Word cover-to-cover each year. Melodee and I had disciplined ourselves to do that each year. Now, alone with God and with His Word before us, we wrestled through our worst nightmares *in His presence.*

Cry often! Faith cries. Often. Faith knows that when things don't go our way – the way we want the script of our lives to unfold – we have to cry out to Jesus, our King and Savior, our Protector and the Lover of our souls. So there, in the darkness and in the light, our eyes leaked the love and fear we felt – often.

Trying to be strong for each other, we also admitted we didn't have all we needed to do that. And that was ok. We gave ourselves permission to cry – in private, together, and in public. Shopping one day for things to help Melodee with pain, I remember being incapable of holding the tears back from my cheeks. And that was ok. The pain in me was unbearable as I watched the monster inside of her eat her life away.

Talk constantly! Having a great relationship was the essential from the day the door to death opened in our lives. Since we talked about everything *before this*, we talked about everything *in this*. Friends carry each other's burdens... listening to the raw emotions, the disjointed words, and the broken hearts... all without judgment or recrimination.

We sought to speak honestly and speak faith into each other. God would do what God would do. But we would not accept anything less than a miracle until He shared His final pronouncement over Melodee's life. So, promises in the Word of God, thoughts from our times alone in prayer, and something we saw on social media, all became part of the soup of the day in our lives.

Hope is a powerful force and we found it to be contagious amid the pain, the doctor's visits, and the treatments. And that hope came from the only One who is the Enabler of Hope. *Melodee had written a book called,* Hope Enabler, *which chronicled the journey she took when our daughter, Hannah, ran away from home. Now she would use those lessons in a much more devastating time of sorrow and fear as we walked together through Death's Shadow Valley.*

Pray much! Day. Night. In the car. When alone. As I shopped and as we ate together. As a family, alone, as a couple… we prayed! Bold prayers, faith-filled prayers, prayers of desperation and prayers of hope flowed from our hearts and lips.

When death comes knocking, it's no time to sleep and relax! It's time to pull out all of the energies and pray. Pray. Pray! Who knows whether God will spare or not? Until we know for sure, we pray for healing and we don't stop as we *"cry out and say, "Jesus, Son of David, have mercy on me!""* (Mark 10:47)

It was in those opening days that my heart began to thaw through prayer. Alone with God I could tell Him my every concern and care. He was tender and gentle with me. He knew where He was going – though at that point I did not – and He knew what He was preparing me for – though I couldn't have imagined it back then if He would have shown me a video of my life now!

My heart began to reshape and reform. My constant prayer was simple. And though some of you may be offended by the rawness of my words, I pray death doesn't come knocking at your door until you are bold enough to come to God's Throne in the transparency of your aching heart. I simply prayed honestly and often, *"Lord, this plan sucks… but I am surrendered. Not my will, but Your's be done."* And God heard my prayer and loved me back to a stronger faith.

Remember people are watching! Something Melodee and I had talked about so much of our married life was this point: People are *always* watching us. When life is good, they dismiss our pleasantries and faith statements. However, *they watch us so closely* when life turns ugly, and we are in over our heads.

Gleaming in their rebellion to God that say, either to themselves or to their friends, *"Now watch all those ridiculous statements about God go out the window. They will act just like the rest of us!"* Yet, for those of us who possess a close walk with God, we understand that even the reality of a death sentence isn't enough to shake our faith. For *"we do not... grieve as others do who have no hope."* (1 Thessalonians 4:13)

So there, in that Oklahoma second-story grandchildren's bedroom, we poured out our hearts to God and to one another. And Melodee reminded me again, *"Honey, people are watching."* To which, I replied, *"We've shown them how to live life for Jesus when everything goes well, now let's show them how to live life when everything goes wrong."* And THAT was the theme of our journey, a journey of faith and hope amidst the pain and suffering, the uncertainty and concerns.

Today, if you are bleeding and wounded, if God didn't answer your prayers just as He didn't answer our prayers for Melodee's healing, then I beg you to read on. Perhaps some of the things God taught me through this horrific chapter in our lives will help and bring healing to you as it has helped and healed me.

I am here to say to you, two plus years since Melodee's transfer to Heaven, that God is good; That His mercies ARE new every morning. That time alone with Him allows for the shaping and healing, the understanding and the hope to grow again!

Taking Action

Consider: When death comes knocking, it's no time to sleep and relax! It's time to pull out all of the energies and pray. Pray. Pray!

Trust: *"I have loved you with an everlasting love; therefore I have continued my faithfulness to you."* **(Jeremiah 31:3)**

Act: *Lord, not my will, but yours be done!*

2

Saying Goodbye

Expressing Yourself Completely Before Their Death

"Even though I walk through the valley of the shadow of death, I will fear no evil,
for you are with me; your rod and your staff, they comfort me."
(Psalm 23:4)

Words are *never* enough. Even though I love to talk, I love to communicate, I love to "play with words" so as to help others understand, words are *never* enough. But words are what we have. They are the gifts God has given us to share the *"thoughts and attitudes of our hearts."* (Hebrews 4:12)

And so, there I was trying to put into words the enormity of all that would have taken me the next three or more decades to share with the Love of my life. My heart. My hopes. My dreams. My fears. My needs. All now laid bare and so, so raw.

Dripping with the blood of these fresh wounds of possible separation from this life, I sought to speak the love and life I enjoyed so much with Melodee each and every time we were together. Tenderness and tears intermingled as we moved forward by faith and retreated in pain to hold each other each day.

Prayers grew more real, more visceral, bolder, and more transparent as the days turned into weeks and the weeks into months. And God grew so much closer in those twists and turns. Death's Shadow Valley is a painful, long, agonizing walk not a just a fancy metaphor. In that valley floor we found the Stream of Life flowing... though many would argue this point. God was *there* just as He promised. And in His presence we *"receive[d] mercy and [found] grace to help in [our] time of need."* (Hebrews 4:16)

Scared and Alone

The fact is that when death comes calling we are all scared. Uncertainty overshadows everything. Plans fly out the window. And we are unsure of how much to share with our loved one who is dying because we don't want to discourage or depress them even more. We truly feel at that moment all alone.

We are fearful to say too much and do even more damage to their already devastated soul.

You don't want to face it. Let's be honest. Who wants to talk about Death's Shadow Valley? Especially when OUR loved one is now having to hike through the rocks and thorns, the snakes and scorpions that lie there? Why would *anyone* want to even *consider* the pain and suffering of such a journey?

Death is a reality for all of us. However, for almost all of us, it is a reality that we *choose to ignore* on purpose. As we celebrate our birthdays each year, we are – perhaps even unwittingly – announcing we are closer to our own personal trek through Death's Shadow Valley. *But for almost all of us, we won't acknowledge that menace in our lives.*

You don't want to take hope away. When Melodee's diagnosis was given, we had both experienced the ravages of cancer with our parents. Three of our four parents had died of the dreadful disease. And while cancer had taken *every one of them* after it came, we served a Mighty God who could create the universe with a word, raise the dead by command, and desired to make people well while He roamed the Earth.

So, why *couldn't* He do it again? Why *wouldn't He* do it again? After all, Jesus Himself promised, *"Therefore I tell you, whatever you ask in prayer, believe that you have received it, and it will be yours."* (Mark 11:24) So why would we talk at length about the diagnosis and bring *doubt* into our hearts. Wouldn't that end the miracle of healing we were praying for?

You don't want to fake it. And yet, there I was realizing that *death could happen* and I wasn't prepared for that! There was so much *to say.* There was so much *to do* yet. I just wanted all of this to *go away!* But it wouldn't. Trips to Houston, Texas for a clearer diagnosis and then back to Los Angeles for treatment simply took a greater toll on each of us every day.

These are the things we had to talk about. I couldn't wake up with a fake smile and a fake faith that simply shrugged everything away. This was *our life* cancer wanted to steal. This was *my wife* cancer wanted to kill. This was *our future* cancer wanted to destroy. (John 10:10)

You don't want to talk about it. And even then, knowing that each conversation could bring fresh pain, fresh grief, fresh wounds, I wanted to just talk about the trivial. *"The weather is cool today." "Did you see there's a sale at the grocery store?" "Gas prices are going up." "What did you want for dinner?"*

But such things are *virtually irrelevant* to the one who is headed into Eternity. I remember like it was yesterday, though it was 1985, my father missing from the front room one night in our home. That was strange because he and my mother sat in front of the television from the time dinner was over until bed almost every night.

When I noticed his absence, I went looking for him and found him in the kitchen. *"Why are you sitting in here?* I asked him. I'll never forget his words that night. *"When you are dying, television just isn't important anymore."* And THAT is the point of this chapter.

You know you need to talk about it. With Eternity staring us coldly in the face, we made a conscious, imperative, bold and painful choice: We chose to speak, to talk, to open up about *everything.* The good things. The bad things. The ugly things. Whether painful or joyful. We talked about it all. We laughed and cried, hugged and kissed, planned and prayed.

You see, *"out of the abundance of the heart his mouth speaks."* (Luke 6:45) We knew we were grieving. We knew we were bleeding. We knew we needed each other. And so, we shared everything… our hopes and dreams, our faith and doubts, our pain and sorrow… *everything.* And from that we learned.

Lessons We Couldn't Learn Elsewhere

In the midst of the plane flights, the doctor's visits, the treatments, the sleeping – yes, Melodee slept a lot more than usual because of the medications – we learned some things that only the imminence of death can produce. And our characters were refined with the hottest fires I've ever known.

Though it's not a journey I would wish on any of us, I know that our faith came out as priceless as gold or silver, refined in the fire. And out of those fires we learned…

How to love each other in the darkness. Death's Shadow Valley is a dark place. And that darkness is magnified by the devil's minions (demons) who constantly whisper about the futility of our situation. While we seek faith, the devil serves death. Like an "all-you-can-eat" buffet, he brings plate after plate, delicacy after delicacy of his poisonous concoctions to our ears, our minds, our hearts, our souls. Soon we are gagging on his gangrene.

However, love sacrifices. (John 3:16; Ephesians 5:25) And now, one of the sacrifices I learned to make was to do *everything necessary* to bring honest hope in God's character to my wife. So, with each piece of good news, I spoke hope. With bad reports I was honest. When things looked bleak, I pointed to Heaven. If the doctor was optimistic, we talked about the grandchildren.

In each encounter, I sacrificed what I *thought would make her happy* with honesty intermingled with faith. In so doing, she loved me all the more and expressed her appreciation for that mixture of love and faith over and over.

How to encourage each other in the uncertainty. Time and again I was overwhelmed with the enormity and awfulness of our situation. As the primary – only – care giver for Melodee from the beginning, I began to fade. My strength has always been extraordinary, but even I have my limits.

In those times Melodee would be the encourager. She would insist I "take a nap" while she did or "go to store" just so I would get a break from her. I don't know how anyone in such a situation could love me so much when her own pain and difficulties were so great. Yet, Death's Shadow Valley can teach us to encourage the other when we need very same encouragement ourselves.

How to pray for each other on our journey. Melodee was always a prayer warrior. She truly spoke to God like Moses spoke with God, *"as a man speaks to his friend."* (Exodus 33:11) But the prospect of death brought us to a different kind of prayer... a more urgent, driven conversation with God *for each other.*

As we prayed, we found ourselves focusing on the other person and on the needs our spouse had. Healing and health for Melodee, strength for me seemed to flow often through our prayers for one another. And in those prayers we found *"the peace of God, which surpasses all understanding"* guarding our hearts and minds. (Philippians 4:7)

How to be even more honest with each other each day. When reports are bad, we all have a tendency to want to hide something, or "shade" the truth with a more acceptable version. We desire to withhold the bitterest parts claiming to love the other person.

Yet, as we moved forward in this process, we discovered that love tells all. It doesn't withhold vital information that later could become reality. And so, when either of us was given a report had a possibility that meant Melodee's death, and the other wasn't there when it was delivered, we shared it all, gruesome as it might be. In so doing, we revealed our absolute trust in one another and for the God *"who is able to do far more abundantly than all that we ask or think, according to the power at work within us."* (Ephesians 3:20)

How to hold on to faith for each other when things were impossible. In times of prolonged illness, exhaustion – physical, mental, emotional, and yes, even spiritual – can take its toll. We were not immune to such times. Few who have endured the grueling torture of long-term illness can understand this reality. For those of us who have a taste of this – and I want to emphasize that we only had *months* with this, not *years* like many – one's faith can be chipped away at so very quietly, just like the work of the tide on the stone cliffs by the seas.

Yet, God was gracious to cause us to realize that our burden, our responsibility, our "grace," was to *"Bear one another's burdens, and so fulfill the law of Christ."* (Galatians 6:2) While each of us realized we could be losing our life partner, Melodee began to turn her attention to me, knowing that she would be with her Lord in Heaven and I would be alone on Earth.

Strengthening one another, we chose consciously and daily to pick each other up. While I'd love to report we did that without failure, life is far messier than that. Though, it is safe to say we chose love and faith over pain and anxiety most all of the time.

How to say goodbye. Since Melodee has this cancer 10 years earlier, our conversations were always salted with the reality of her death. The first time around she had picked my future wife, to my acceptance of her choice. This time around, when the doctor said there would be no cure, we simply spoke of every aspect of our lives and that especially included Heaven.

When her end in Heaven was certain, I left her with messages to take to family and friends and images of the joy she would experience from my reading of God's words. And she told me of how to live life *without her* and that I was to

LIVE my life without her. And we said goodbye with honesty and love. We didn't "sugar-coat" things. We "love-coated" everything. And because of that, I can say honestly that my regrets are so few they do not matter.

Today I cannot emphasize that if your loved one is still alive but struggling with a terminal disease, *express yourself completely before their death.* Leave nothing unsaid. Talk about everything. Part as dearest friends, just as you were meant to be throughout life. You will never regret it and they will thank you for eternity for it.

Taking Action

Consider: With Eternity staring you coldly in the face, make a conscious, imperative, bold and painful choice: Chose to speak, to talk, and to open up about *everything*.

Trust: *"Even though I walk through the valley of the shadow of death, I will fear no evil, for you are with me; your rod and your staff, they comfort me."* (Psalm 23:4, ESV)

Act: *Leave nothing unsaid. Talk about everything. Part as dearest friends, just as you were meant to be throughout life.*

3

How Grief Works

Understanding the Tide, Drowning, Rip Currents, and Learning to Swim

"But we do not want you to be uninformed, brothers, about those who are asleep, that you may not grieve as others do who have no hope."
(1 Thessalonians 4:13)

Convulsing with uncontrollable sobs of incredible loss and emptiness, I sat on my bed for who knows how long after Melodee's promotion. While I had been at the entrance of this Valley before with grandparents, parents, aunts, uncles and other relatives, nothing like this had ever enveloped me with such overwhelming power and force.

Having been a pastor for decades allowed me some advantage, as I knew this was normal and needed. So, there I sat pouring out my grief with only the hospice nurse comforting and rubbing my back in careful concern. There, in the darkness of my bedroom at 3:05 am that Saturday morning, alongside the "tent" of my life-long partner, I simply let the sorrow and emotion take me wherever it wanted.

Grief Is Like the Tide

Grief is a strange and dangerous beast. The best metaphor I can come up with is that it is like the tide at the ocean. While the person on the shore sees it come and go, it isn't until one is *in the water* and *feeling its effects* that the horrible power and danger engulfs the senses and invokes the terror.

Grief overpowers. Like that summer at the beach so long ago when the tide started to pull me farther and farther from shore, as I cried my eyes out in the wee hours of her departure, I realized I was slowly, unexplainably, being pulled in a direction I had no desire to go.

Yet, there was no way to get back. She was on Heaven's shore and I was still here. A great gulf was fixed between us – the temporal and the eternal. One moment we were together, the next pulled apart, not to again be reunited in this life. Feelings of helplessness and anxiety quickly overpowered my senses.

Grief suffocates. Perhaps the greatest terror that comes with grief is the inability to breathe. Yes, I was still taking air into my lungs *but it felt like* I couldn't catch my breath. Like being submerged in the depths of the ocean, unsure which way is up, I felt like I would never survive despite each attempt to crawl back to the surface.

How I wanted to regain my equilibrium. I just wanted things to *go back to normal.* Dark thoughts flooded my mind. Loneliness pulled me further into the abyss. Feelings of despair started to tear at my soul. I thought I was prepared for this. I thought I was stronger than this. And yet, there I was... aching, bleeding, broken, and lost in the grip of the monster I now know so well as grief.

Grief terrorizes. Unlike the tide, grief can sneak up when I least expect it. Opening a box with things I needed to sort for taxes I found Melodee's handwritten notes on the zip lock bags she used for our receipts as well as notations in the checkbook ledgers. But perhaps the worst day so far was when I found the stash of cards she'd written to me this past year. Notes of love and affection, which brought such happiness months ago, not brought dreadful sorrow... aching torment... darkness.

Like a bully on the playground, each card taunted me to read it. And with each read, the tears flowed again. The sobs of grief and loss overtook my heart and soul. How I missed this woman! Yet, I couldn't NOT read them! Hence, the terror. Grief pulled me back, goading me to remember all I had lost. Gloom sought to destroy me.

Would to God that this tide would only come on the first day of our despair. What a world it would be if grief lasted only 24 hours. Then, with a new day and a new sunrise, it would depart never to be thought of or experienced again. Would to God... but it doesn't happen like that.

You see, I have also learned that *grief is like a sniper.* It sits up high and waits for our most vulnerable times, often when we are getting back to life and starting to experience some form of happiness. Then it shoots us down, often tearing open a gaping wound as it rips us apart all over again. Grief seems to delight in doing this.

Once, years after my father, Louis, died of smoking-related cancer, I can remember being in a Smart and Final grocery store in Southern California shopping with Melodee. As she was in one part of the store, I headed down the candy aisle. There, on the shelf were bags of Brach's Spicettes jelly candy, my dad's "omnipresent" favorite candy! I can never remember a time when he didn't have a bag in the car, at work, or at home.

Crumbling into a pile of Jell-O, I simply fell to the floor crying my eyes out in the candy aisle. Fortunately for me, it was a slow day for candy and I had a long cry. Finally, Melodee had finished her shopping and came looking for me. Seeing me, she sat down beside me and held me until I could regain control. *Years had passed since my dad's death* and there I was balling like a baby over a bag of candy. *Grief takes its time and hurts as much if not more when it arrives again.*

Grief passes. If you have been walking through the Valley of the Shadow of Death for a while, you are no doubt familiar with this truth. Like the tide, grief passes – as long as we keep swimming, keeping our head above water. As the day dawned that first Saturday of Melodee's home-going, I realized what Jeremiah had written some 2,600 years ago was still true: *"The steadfast love of the Lord never ceases; his mercies never come to an end; they are new every morning; great is your faithfulness."* (Lamentations 3:22–23)

While things were not "all better" that morning, hope began to stir with the sunrise. God still loved me more than I could ever understand or experience. He was continuing to give me so much of what I didn't deserve – I lived in a house where the family had taken us in when we were homeless, they allowed Melodee to come home to die *in their home!* And now, they were there, with tears flowing down their cheeks, holding me, hugging me, speaking life into me! This new morning – this first morning without the love of my life at my side – again reminded me that *His mercies are new every morning and His faithfulness to me is greater than I could ever expect!*

Swimming in the Tide

Danger and death are realities when the tide starts to take control of us in the ocean. We have *to choose to live.* Nothing could be closer to reality when it comes to grief as well. What we do and how quickly we react will determine whether we slip into danger or swim out to safety.

As I wrap up this chapter, I want to share some very personal and practical actions I took, and still take, when grief rears its ugly head and seeks to destroy my life.

Stop. Grief loves to confuse and befuddle. As it seeks to overwhelm your senses, stop. Simply choose *not* to go with the flow. Say it out loud if you need to: "Stop it! I will not go with this flow of discouragement that leads to death! I choose to live life! I choose to accept God's love! I choose to see His new mercies every day!"

Our choices determine a great deal of our destiny. Every choice turns us down a path. As Jesus reminded us, there are, in reality, only two paths: Life and death (See John 10:10). For me, each day, I choose the life Jesus promised me: *"I came that they may have life and have it abundantly."* (John 10:10)

Surrender. When I knelt at my bedside the night Melodee was promoted, I said, *"Lord, this plan sucks, but I am **SURRENDERED**. Whatever you do is right. I trust you. Show me your will. Show me what's next. I only want to please you."*

It is a prayer I prayed for weeks and still do pray. I am quite sure my father in heaven smiles and rejoices at my simple trust in His hidden plan that He is unfolding. While I don't understand it all yet, and may never until eternity, I know this: *Whatever God does is right even in the darkness.* And I trust Him because God is with me! As a result, He is restoring my joy and my hope daily as a result of my trust and my choice to move forward with Him!

Seek. I could not walk through this Valley if it wasn't for my close friendship with God. Each morning I get up and open my Bible, listening for His voice of love, reassurance, and direction. Then, I ask for His guidance as I pray. I ask specific questions, like: *Lord, how do I make the rest of my life the best of my life?* As I first asked this question, God began to form some ideas in my heart based on *the yearly calendar* Melodee always bought. So, I began to ask...

- What would I put on this *New Year's* calendar?
- Who would it include?
- What activities would fill the pages?
- Will I choose to live a joyful life this year?
- Am I ready to embrace the new chapter God has before me?
- Will I look to the future and not be stuck in the past?

Dozens of questions like this were flowing through my mind in those first months. It probably seems obvious to you that *I can't live this year (or any year) like I lived the last 38.* Without Melodee, life is going to be very different. So, I asked (and still ask), *"What do You want for me next, God?"*

If God has answers to these questions, then He surely wants to share them with us. And since He wants to share those answers with us, I began to realize that exciting answers were ahead. More about that later in the book!

Support. Grief loves the shadows. It loves to get us to live in those shadows. Discouragement, despair, and a will to die follow a life lived in the shadows.

As I already mentioned, my LA family – the Sariles who have taken us and now me in as family – are essential to my healing. Without their love and support, conversation and cajoling, I would be a mess.

For years, Melodee and I have built an incredible network of men and women throughout Southern California, people we have poured our lives into. Now, in my season of need, they have come flocking to my rescue. I choose to accept almost every invitation if possible – a lesson I learned from my Aunt Phoebe after her husband, Otto, died.

If you are on my Facebook feed, you will see the food, fun, fellowship posted often. Eating, laughing, and doing life in the light is what not only keeps grief at bay but brings life, healing and wholeness.

If you have locked yourself in your home, unlock the door! If you have surrendered to the shadows, escape! Call a friend. Ask to go to coffee or a meal. Choose life! It's how we heal and how we defeat grief!

<table>
<tr><td>

Taking Action

Consider: Doing life in the light is what not only keeps grief at bay but brings life, healing and wholeness.

Trust: *"I came that they may have life and have it abundantly."* (John 10:10)

Act: *Lord, how do I make the rest of my life the best of my life?*

</td></tr>
</table>

4

The Human Touch

Longing for the Affection You Once Thrived Under

"Let him kiss me with the kisses of his mouth!
For your love is better than wine;" (Song of Solomon 1:2)

After decades of tenderness and affection, its end was devastating. A gentle hand on the shoulder, a hug in the hall, and a warm kiss were all part and parcel of our daily routine as a married couple.

We often don't realize how much we touch one another as a couple until we no longer are able to do so. Of course, when we go away on an overnight trip or for business for a few days it becomes a reality. Yet, there is always the anticipation of our return, their warm embrace, and the touch of the one whom we love.

And then, once they are gone forever, there is *no one.* So few speak of this that it has been my discovery that most who have experienced it are embarrassed to talk about it. And while so few will talk about it, everyone who walks through Death's Shadow Valley experiences it.

We experience the pain and the struggle of being alone. There's no one to hold, no one to come home to. No one brushes their hand against your face and asks us, *"How was your day, baby?"* In these moments pain overwhelms. All we want is someone to touch, someone who tenderly shows you that they care. But we don't want *someone.* We want *that* someone, that *one person* that we have spent our lives with. And now they're gone… forever.

Aching for Affection

We are told that men ache more than women for affection. It's been my experience that we *all* long for touch. Even Jesus, when he was going to heal people who had been sent "out of the camp" in Israel because of their contagious disease understood this. Like the man with leprosy, a contagious skin disease, *"Jesus stretched out his hand and touched him, saying, "I will; be clean."* *And immediately his leprosy was cleansed."* (Matthew 8:3) Jesus understood the power of touch and He would often touch those who had not been touched by others during the whole time of their infirmity.

And now, so much more as I struggled with the emotions of grief, I discovered that I was struggling with the *affections of grief.* Isolation is a very difficult condition to experience. It's not like you don't have friends. It's not like they don't care about you for they often do care very, very much.

The reality is that you're looking for someone whom you can touch and feel their heart and soul – *that* heart and soul that loves you with an everlasting love. And while that touch would be inappropriate in any other setting, in our marriage relationship it was part of the fertilizer that grew our love for one another. But that isn't possible right now.

Yet, today, we need someone to express their love in a physical, appropriate manner. Of course, this is the value of close family. Those who live closest to us can hold us, pay us on the back, embrace us when we are struggling, and just touch or hold our hand in the quiet of a pause in the conversation.

There is something visceral, something essential, and something almost undefinable about the touch of your loved one. You know what I mean, don't you? Melodee had a way of sneaking up behind me and just putting her hands on my shoulders. She may not have lingered long, but it was her way of saying, *"I'm here. I have your back. I love you."*

We are told that touch is the very first sense that is developed. For those of us who lose the love of our lives, we can very well understand why God made it that way. In the touch of our mate we sense emotions that cause us to respond or react depending on their nature.

Filling the Void

Whether it was late at night and I lay in bed alone, or during the day working at my desk, the ache to be touched was ever present after Melodee's promotion to Heaven. What *would* I do about it? What *could* I do to meet a very biblical need in a very biblical manner?

Shake hands often. Remember, touch is a communication device. It allows you to tell others how you feel and it allows them to reciprocate. I can remember in the early days after Melodee's departure that I would often just reach out my hand. I'm still amazed at the number of people who would grab my hand and instead of shaking it would pull me to them and give me a hug.

It seems that people instinctively understand that we are in pain when they touch us. It is a God given response to embrace us so they can help melt away our pain. Time and again, in many different locations with many different kinds of people I would experience the same thing. Touch always communicates. So if you're going through a difficult time right now, and you're in grief, and if You don't know what to do, just reach your hand out and allow someone to touch it, to shake it, and watch what happens.

Put your hand on their shoulder. A lot of times when we're aching for some sort of affection, simply putting a hand on the shoulder of a friend can change everything. Now I want to be upfront and say that it's important that you choose your friends carefully. I would tell you that this has to be a person you trust. And I would even go further and say that it should be someone of the same sex. We don't want to miscommunicate at this moment.

However, simply walking up to one of my friends one day, I placed my hand on the shoulder. We were in a group that was having a conversation in the parking lot after worship. And since I was not part of the conversation yet, I simply put my hand on the shoulder of the friend next to me as a delaying tactic before saying anything. What happened next was astounding. He simply picked my hand off his shoulder, turned around to me, and gave me a hug.

You see, everyone knows you've lost your loved one. And they know that they want to be able to help us in some way. They simply don't know how. When we make the first step, the step of touch, so much changes so quickly. But again I want to remind you to choose your friends carefully. These are people who know you. These are people who love you. These are people who appreciate the pain you're in right now.

And with each touch, with each response, healing comes. The void is filled–for a moment anyway, and life breaks into our darkness once again. It is a refreshing, surprising, and, I'll admit it, addicting feeling!

Be honest with family. While many may not understand what we're talking about, we can be sure that if our family is close to us they will get it. Telling them that from time to time you just need a hug without asking, that you need some affection physically, will go a long ways in bringing healing and help inner times of need.

Living with my pastor and his family during Melodee's sickness, death and afterwards could have been difficult in this area had they not been *my Los Angeles family.* Along the way a hug, a hand on my shoulder, and just a gentle touch as they passed me in the hall did so much to restore my equilibrium. How I thank God for the gift of touch and the people who choose to embrace when we are writhing in pain, bleeding with emotions, and seeking for some semblance of normalcy again.

Remember, your family has walked down this path with you. While their pain may not be as great as yours because you lost your spouse, they are not without sorrow themselves. One of the wonderful creations of God is family. It allows us to experience in microcosm what God calls us to experience within the church: *"Rejoice with those who rejoice, weep with those who weep. Live in harmony with one another."* (Romans 12:15–16)

Give a friend a hug. During that first year when my emotions and my affections were bleeding a lot, I would often walk up to close friends and just tell them, *"I need a hug."* They understood that there was nothing sensual or sexual about it. They understood that I wasn't being weird. I was just in pain.

A lot of times I would just, when the moment was appropriate, give a guy a hug. As men, we like to give each other bear hugs once in a while and see who can crack the other person's rib. Of course I'm joking a little bit, but not completely. It's a man's thing. It's a competition at times. But it's a wonderful way to demonstrate to friends that we care about the other.

I remember one night, after small group, the discussion must have triggered some emotions and some pain. Perhaps people could see it on my face. But on that particular night I remember my small group, without any prompting from me, just came and hugged me. Several of them said, *"I can see you need a hug."*

Are we really that transparent? I believe we are. And I believe that the God who loves us, the God who left us behind, the God do has a plan for us, is reminding us that *there will be life again.* That one-day there will be *someone* in our lives again – if we'll simply open that door and be open to act when it arrives.

28

So give a friend a hug. Ask for one. They'll understand. And you'll heal faster as result of that hug. I want you to trust me here. And as you are appropriate, God is there to strengthen you, to heal you, to breathe life into you once again.

Remain pure and godly. Now in all of this discussion, I want to be sure that you understand the bottom line. And that simply is, God is watching. God knows our thoughts and he knows the intentions of our hearts. (Hebrews 4:12) Receiving affection from friends and family is not an excuse to be immoral. It is a process toward healing. To abuse this gift from other people, whether by what we think or by what we do, is something that God himself will deal with in our lives. Our task is to remain pure. We should remember the words of God himself as He expresses them through King Solomon…

"The end of the matter; all has been heard. Fear God and keep his commandments, for this is the whole duty of man. For God will bring every deed into judgment, with every secret thing, whether good or evil." (Ecclesiastes 12:13–14)

These are sobering words. And so they should be. In the swirling emotions of our affections, we can be sure that the devil would rather destroy us than allow God to heal us. Because we have lost our loved one and we are writhing in pain is no excuse for losing our character and our Christ likeness.

So if today as you ache for some affection, you have permission to reach out and touch someone appropriately. Shake a hand. Touch a friend. Be transparent. And remember God is watching. He longs for you to be whole. And He's given us the gift of touch to bring us back to the land of the living.

Taking Action

Consider: God has given us the gift of touch to bring us back to the land of the living…

Trust: *"Jesus stretched out his hand and touched him, saying, "I will; be clean." And immediately his leprosy was cleansed."* (Matthew 8:3)

Act: *Reach out and touch someone appropriately. Shake a hand. Touch a friend. Be transparent.*

5

Disconnectedness

Comprehending the Enormity of the Fact that,
"I've Been Disconnected from My Soul-Mate"

"This at last is bone of my bones and flesh of my flesh; she shall be called Woman, because she was taken out of Man." Therefore a man shall leave his father and his mother and hold fast to his wife, and they shall become one flesh." (Genesis 2:23–24)

Sitting in our recliners at home together, we would often finish each other's sentences. From time to time, while resting and not having said anything for a long while, one of us would just start chuckling. Turning to the other, we'd say, "Were you thinking about this?" Most often the other would reply, "Yes!"

I often, tell people, "We weren't just *married*. We weren't *happily* married. We were a symbiosis." When you adore someone like I adored Melodee and vice versa, we longed for each other's presence. We sought to *know* each other deeply. Frequently I would say, "I'm THE leading authority on that woman. I know what she's thinking or, at least, how she will react at any given time."

That connection – that spiritual, visceral, intellectual, emotional, connection became so much a part of me I often didn't realize it was there. Truly, *the two became one.* While we were totally different in so many ways, we were one. We functioned as one, sought the counsel of the other before we made almost every decision, and longed to talk with each other constantly. (We would Facebook Messenger each other while working at our desks – in the same room!)

If I was traveling or in my office at work; we would message or text each other all throughout the day *because we missed each other.* At home, out shopping, or on a date, we would talk constantly, despite the fact that we probably already knew what the other was going to say or how they were going to respond.

Disconnection

And then, it was… gone! On the night she was promoted to Glory, Melodee and I talked a lot. Though it was hard for her to get her breath and her breathing was labored, she wasn't about to disconnect one moment before she had to. She asked me when the girls were coming; Hannah was driving the 1,500 miles from Texas and would arrive around 9 am that morning and Tabitha was flying home from her dream vacation in London and would be home around dinnertime.

She longed to worship the Lord so she sang. And then, perhaps in a reality check, she told me she wanted to go to Heaven before me. When I told her I thought she was going to get her wish, she got quiet. Then she started laughing *at me,* since she was about to beat me to the golden avenues of the New Jerusalem.

When she breathed her last breath, I sensed it almost immediately. Perhaps, if you are grieving the loss of your spouse like we are, you know what I mean? It was there one moment and then, it was gone.

That familiar, warm, life-giving link simply disappeared, much like a dropped cell call. I no longer had service with the one who made life so much easier, so much more vibrant, and so much more vital.

What surprised me the most was the ache it left. While I know it was ethereal, an otherworldly gift from our good, good Father, its absence hurt! It still does. Whether I'm in the kitchen making a meal or in the car driving to an appointment it is noticeably and shakably absent. Sometimes I simply have to stop and recover. At other times, I realize I don't know how to make a decision without her. Or, in the midst of something joy-filled I can't *hear her joy in my head and heart.* Not the audible sound, mind you. I'm speaking of the inner song of her presence. It no longer plays as the soundtrack of my heart… and it hurts.

Dealing with the Silence

Along the way, I've discovered that I can choose to deal with this new and heart-breaking reality in one of two ways. I can deal with it to my destruction or I can choose hope. So, on a daily – sometimes hourly – basis, I choose hope! After all, our God is THE God of Hope! As the Psalmist rightly declares: *"Why are you cast down, O my soul, and why are you in turmoil within me? Hope in God; for I shall again praise Him, my Rescue!"* (Psalm 42:5, adapted)

Never look downward! As we said in chapter three, danger and death are realities when our grief starts to take control of us. The lure of the abyss grows when we nurture its thoughts. The darker the gloom, the quicker our doom.

Apart from the hope of God's words in our lives, grief's despair grows more powerful. When explaining the power of hope, the psalmist prays, *"Remember your word to your servant, in which you have made me hope. This is my comfort in my affliction, that your promise gives me life."* (Psalm 119:49–50)

Look upward! One of the key reasons to read God's Word, our Bible, every day is the darkness-dispelling authority is possesses. On a dark night at the four-month anniversary of Melodee's home going and promotion, I felt totally and completed entwined in the cords of despair. Letting my LA family know and messaging a few friends to pray, I battled with the greatest darkness I had experienced to that point.

With Scripture on my walls, I knelt in prayer, praying the promises and insights God had given me over the weeks and months before. Only then did the darkness begin to part. As I prayed, thoughts like this came to my heart and lips: *"My soul longs for your rescue; I hope in your word. My eyes long for your promise; I ask, "When will you comfort me?""* (Psalm 119:81–82, adapted)

As the tears flowed and I opened my aching heart to the One who alone does wonders (Judges 13:19) the comfort I sought started to flow. God began to rescue me from the pit my heart had fallen into. The despair began to leave and by morning I was much better.

Look inward. If we want to be dreadfully honest, which is the only way to heal, we have to admit that feeling sorry for ourselves is just plain selfish. Our focus is too much, "Me, me, me!" If we are children of the Most High God and our allegiance is to Jesus Christ, we will have to fall to our knees tonight beside our bed and utter those now-famous but then-torturous words of Jesus, *"Not my will, but yours, be done."* (Luke 22:42)

This was perhaps the greatest test of my life. Will I utter those words, not from my head, but from my heart? As I did the week we discovered Melodee would not recover, as I did again last night, and as I have done every night in between, I find great relief in those words.

Have you *listened* to those words lately? If not, take a moment to read them out loud *until* you hear them. *"Not my will, but yours, be done."* (Luke 22:42) Now, say it like you *mean it* as it pertains to your grief, your loss. Now, say it again! Each time you read it emphasize a different word.

Until I can *surrender* to the plan of God and *say so* with conviction, I will not enjoy, *"the peace of God, which surpasses all understanding."* (Philippians 4:7) As I read and reread this passage, I discover that grief is an issue of my heart and head. Listen to Paul finish that verse... *"The peace of God, which surpasses all understanding, will guard your hearts and your minds in Christ Jesus."* (Philippians 4:7)

As you look inward, after you have looked upward, you will discover that it is the application of our faith that brings health and healing to our shredded soul. As I am fond to say, *"Our knowing isn't growing until our knowing is showing."* There is no greater verification that Jesus Christ is true and that our faith is authentic than when we go through such a catastrophic loss and stand in genuine peace.

Look outward! One of the greatest ways to deal with the silence is to reconnect with others. God made us to be connected, not just as a couple or as a family, but as the family of God. When you look over the dozens of "one another" instructions in the New Testament it becomes very hard to justify a life lived alone in the shadows of one's home, even if we are suffering from a dreadful loss. In fact, to be honest, for the Christian to become a social hermit is tantamount to rebellion to God's direct words of instruction.

Coming to grips with the fact that God intended us to do life together; I chose to accept invitations to events and coffee. Soon, I was making calls and connections to do things together. Because of Melodee's prolonged illness, we weren't able to do things with people as much as we wanted to. Now I had the time. Would I choose to have the attitude? I chose life!

When people come up to me now they say things like, "I see by your Facebook posts that you are quite busy. It looks like you're having fun!" *And, I am!* God is restoring the joy of my heart and healing it – one coffee, one meal, one reconnected relationship at a time.

In the silence of being disconnected from Melodee I am learning that God does bring peace. He wants to bring me so much more. However, I must *trust Him.* I must choose to believe the truth of these words of the Lord God Almighty, the One who loves me and sent His Son, Jesus, to prove that love by dying in my place on the hellish cross: *"I will guide you along the best pathway for your life. I will advise you and watch over you."* (Psalm 32:8, NLT)

Trust Him, look upward, look inward, and look outward! All the resources of Heaven are at our disposal to bring healing to our shredded souls.

Taking Action

Consider: The darker the gloom, the quicker our doom.

Trust: *"I will guide you along the best pathway for your life. I will advise you and watch over you."* **(Psalm 32:8, NLT)**

Act: Choose hope!

6

The Longing for Their Presence

Wanting to be with Someone

*"On my bed by night I sought him whom my soul loves;
I sought him, but found him not."* (Song of Solomon 3:1)

It was the first Resurrection Day after Melodee's promotion and I was doing fine. Pastor Bryan had graciously asked me to speak that Sunday for worship. We had so much planned that day as the church gathered, including a quinceañera!

Everything was going smoothly. There I was greeting members and guests, laughing and rejoicing in the goodness of God. And then it happened. One of my well-meaning friends felt compelled to remind me that this was *my first Resurrection Day* without Melodee.

Minutes before the service, as I looked down at the Facebook post, I felt my soul being sucked into the vortex of darkness and there was little I could do about it. All I wanted at that moment was to have Melodee at my side. Alas, that would never be. To make matters worse, a dear friend and fellow traveler on Death's Shadow Valley, Gigi, who had been so helpful so often and who was planning to come to the service got sick that morning. I felt like I'd been gut-punched and there was no one who understood how to help me. Surrounded by friends I felt so alone.

Aching at the Emptiness

Somehow, by God's grace, I got through the message, my mind totally darkened by the despair I felt pulling at me. I'd been here before and I am sure I will be there again. What was so incredibly shocking was how sudden it came from an innocuous and genuinely caring comment made from a heart that cares.

Throughout my journey of grief and recovery I have felt the disconnectedness as I explained in the last chapter. However, this was so much more. This was *visceral.* I ached from the emptiness. I hurt, almost to tears, all day and into the night. Surrounded by my friends and church family, I couldn't shake the gloom.

One of my dear friends at the church, Marisa's dad, Gabriel, noticed it first. He pulled me aside in the afternoon as we celebrated his wedding anniversary and asked, "Are you ok brother? Did something happen?" When I shared that it had, I felt his love and care immediately. Yet, the melancholy wouldn't leave me. Hours passed and amidst those who truly care deeply for me, I... felt... so... *alone*.

It is hard to describe the pain to those who haven't lost their spouse or close family member. This ache is so different from anything else we have ever felt. The freshness of our pain, coupled with the brokenness of our souls, make for a lethal and overwhelming combination of emotions.

To a lesser degree it happens daily, or at least every other day at this point (about five months after Melodee's promotion). *I just longed for her.* I longed to hear her voice, sense her presence, and even tell me to take out the trash or clean up my mess. It's just so lonely without her.

Dealing with the Darkness

One of the key issues I have discovered, that I have mentioned before and I will mention again and again is this, we MUST connect with people as we grieve. There is nothing godly about becoming a hermit! In fact, retreating into our own gloom is sin, a gross violation of the dozens of the "one-another" passages in the New Testament. We can't do life alone and we surely cannot do grief alone.

One of the early principles I learned in life is that there is power in numbers. *"And though a man might prevail against one who is alone, two will withstand him—a threefold cord is not quickly broken."* (Ecclesiastes 4:12) What's true of physical enemies is equally true of emotional ones, especially grief!

So, I did what I am telling you. I began to reach out. I spoke with several close friends who listen and have my heart in their hands. Each could see the deep pain in my eyes and knew I was in trouble. If you get to know me well, you know I love to joke and kid around. Sometimes I think I missed my calling as a comedian. However, each of those I spoke with could see this wasn't the time or mood I was in, even though each can parry jovial swords with me anytime.

Find that one person. With each conversation, the darkness of that first Resurrection Day began to recede. When I need the guidance of a clear eye and the reminder of the vision of God for my life, I speak with Pastor Bryan. When I need a compassionate ear that will listen and share wisdom and insight, I often speak with Pastor Bryan's wife, Marisa. At other times I need the insight and affirmation of my son, Ryne. When I need to be buoyed in the midst of the battle, I go to the always joyful and caring Monina, a lady in our church that draws everyone in like a hen draws her chicks. However, this night – this first Resurrection Day without Melodee – my heart was still bleeding and I needed someone who had experienced my pain and knew me well enough to speak life into me.

Late in the evening – when she should have been in bed resting for work the next day and knowing she was trying to recover from her illness – I texted my friend, Gigi, who couldn't make it to church because of sickness and told her I was in agony. Despite her sickness, we messaged back and forth until almost midnight. She started with these words; "I'm here for you, always. Everything will be just fine."

Listen to their words. Her counsel was compassionate and powerful. She knew how to provide the surgery needed to cut away the tendrils of terror that had so painfully attached themselves to my heart. Like a skilled surgeon she spoke of Melodee. In caps, she wrote, "Remember, she married you because she saw something in you… God showed her your strength and heart. She may be gone physically, however, keep in mind you provided her with the best years of her life. She was happy here and now she's watching over you to make sure you're happy and do exactly what she's asked of you."

Then, like a surgeon's scalpel, knowing who I am and what I needed to hear, she wrote these words that released the last tentacle of this terrible toxin. She said, "So you better get to it mister. You have graduations, weddings, and souls to save. Tap into your inner strength and live your best life. You've got this."

Do you have someone who can speak life into you when you need it most? Do you have *several* someones? I will say it again – and again - there is nothing godly about becoming a hermit! We MUST connect with people as we grieve. As Gigi spoke life into me that night, so have Pastor Bryan, Marisa, Ryne, Monina,

Ofel, and several others along this journey. I *depend* on them to do so. I know whom I need at any given moment. Do you have that support group around you? If not, you need to get to it. Reread the action steps in chapter 3. Then, make some calls! Build your network of support.

Trust their care. Here's the key. Do you trust the person you are talking to? When I speak with Pastor Bryan, I know he has my best in mind. Marisa always wants me to heal and sacrifices her time to make that happen. Ryne longs for dad to be happy and do ministry well again. Ofel sees a day when I minister to thousands and wants to help me get to that place. Monina longs for me to enjoy life yet again and Gigi holds my heart with tender care as only one who has walked through the Valley of the Shadow of Death can do.

I trust them all! Without them, each of them and all of them, I would be a mess. However, with them, because I trust they have my best interests at heart, I am healing and I have hope.

Thank God for them. Like that night of that first Resurrection Day without Melodee, when I stayed up late praying for Gigi and thanking God for her sacrifice to bring life into the dark death invading my heart, I am often praying more and more for those who speak life into me with each new encounter.

Each night I pray for Pastor Bryan, Marisa, Ryne, Monina, Ofel, and others because they are gracious gifts from God. Asking for their prosperity, their health, and for futures of success, I plead with my God, the One who has loved me so much as to walk with me in this new season of life. I want the rest of my life to be the best of my life, a prayer I frequently pray for these men and women as well.

God is so good when we will but allow Him to insert His agents of care and compassion into our lives. But that takes the first step on our part: To make the call or send the text and be painfully transparent, as I did that first Resurrection night without Melodee. Will you do it? Now?

Taking Action

Consider: We can't do life alone and we surely cannot do grief alone.

Trust: *"And though a man might prevail against one who is alone, two will withstand him—a threefold cord is not quickly broken."* **(Ecclesiastes 4:12)**

Act: Make the call or send the text and be painfully transparent!

7

Loneliness

Realizing Friends and Family Can't Fill the Void

*"Turn to me and be gracious to me, for I am lonely and afflicted.
The troubles of my heart are enlarged; bring me out of my distresses."*
(Psalm 25:16–17)

Loneliness is one of the worst conditions I've ever experienced in my life. It is amazing to me that as much as I long to be connected with people socially, the absence of my life partner could spoil almost any situation I was in if I was not careful and mindful of that reality.

In the weeks and months following Melodee's death, even when I was in the worship service with my good friends, my church family, things seemed different. While people sat around me and next to me, it felt like I was all alone. I knew they cared. I knew they were praying. And I knew that they would do whatever they could to help me recover and heal.

The problem was that they could not do what only God can do. God heals broken hearts. And God can heal your broken heart. But in what seems to be an oxymoron, God uses the people who cannot heal our broken heart to help heal our broken heart. Let me explain.

Being Cut On the Broken Pieces

As we have said before, grief is a monster. It doesn't play fair. It seems to delight in drawing blood from our already shredded emotional wounds. With each day of Melodee's absence, life seemed to produce a new way for me to hurt.

We are bleeding within. No more conversations. No more giggling. There was no more banter. The teasing was gone. All of those things that created this intimacy on a spiritual, psychological, the emotional level were gone. The one who gave their soul to me no longer existed within me. And every day in so many ways I was bleeding.

Our friends, and even our family members, care so very much. They love us. They aren't sure how to help us but they long to do so. And so they call, they drop by, and they invite us into their lives. By their words they tell us about their love. By their actions they show how real that love is.

Still, with every call, text, or visit, we seem to realize the absence of our loved one more. Watching Pastor Bryan and Marissa come to check on me reminded me there is no one to walk with me through life anymore. People would come and ask, "How are you doing?" But in their question I was reminded again of the void in my soul. Where, "two had become one," now one was trying to exist alone.

We are lost in the darkness. When was the last time you were physically lost? Was it when you were a child? Perhaps you were driving to a new location and the directions you had were not adequate to get you there. Do you remember how you felt?

What did you do? Did you call for help? Did you stop? Did you struggle? You see, how we respond to being lost in the darkness is a part of our spiritual journey and our character. When grief rears its ugly head, some of us panic! I'm not one to panic often, but when I am lost physically, I do get emotionally concerned.

It's not our friends and family members' fault that we're so lonely. And it surely is not their fault that they compound the loneliness by their visits and care. It is just a reality. We are lost in the darkness of our grief as we wander Death's Shadow Valley.

We are wondering what's happening to us. So many times people suffering from the loss of their loved one have asked me, "Why did this happen?" "What did I do to cause the death of my spouse?" "Is God mad at me?" These questions reveal a serious crisis of faith. They call into question basic truths that the Bible answers clearly. Yet in the darkness we don't necessarily remember God has a plan. People have an expiration date. God loves us.

Confusion is often the state of our minds when grief attacks. Unless our spouse was very old, questions thrive in the soil of uncertainty concerning their death. "Why was Melodee taken so young?" "As a vibrant prayer warrior, wasn't she needed for her family?" "What will I do next?" "Is God done with me?" "What does God want from me now? "How will I know what that is?"

We are struggling four balance every day. You know these questions… and the dozens of others that grab a hold of us while we are driving, when we're getting something to eat, and even while we're watching our favorite television show! They will keep us off-balance all day long if we allow them to.

And again, it is in these times we realize how integral our life partner was to our day-to-day activities. It was Melodee's thought, Melodee's comment, Melodee's advice, Melodee's smile that brought stability to my world. Like training wheels on the young child's bicycle, Melodee's constant interactions allowed me to travel through life more smoothly.

Healing Broken Hearts

Healing is often a process that takes longer to happen then we can imagine or desire. And just like a physical wound, we may not see any progress for a while. Grief is a major trauma to our soul and it takes a season to heal from. While we will not heal quickly, we will heal if we remember at we are lost in the darkness and Jesus is the light that leads us out of Death's Shadow Valley.

First Aid for Our Wounds. I do not know how many times something or someone reopened my wounds of sorrow and grief. I did not count or keep track of the times I sat alone in tears wondering when the ache would go away. But I do know that every morning I would rise and open God's Word because in those words I found life and health and healing.

It was just two months and 11 days after Melodee's promotion that God reminded me, *"I am the LORD, your healer."* (Exodus 15:26) while I could not stop the pain, My God could heal. God *would* heal my soul and I *would* be whole again. In that season, the great physician applied the first aid, the bandages, and the prescription for my recovery. He will do the same for you.

God's love is overwhelming. God longs for our restoration. Trust him today with your healing. Cry out to the Doctor of your soul… King Jesus. Open His Word each day. Use the reading schedule at the end of this book to help guide you as you read.

Often my prayers were just mimicking back to Him the words of God from my daily reading. I would be telling Him that I trusted him, telling Him that I believed him, telling Him I knew His character was good. And each day a new place was touched by a new medicine from His words of encouragement, power, and love. He will do the same for you. Just open your heart and open your Bible and cry out to Jesus!

Light in Our Darkness

We have to remember that in our darkness Jesus is the light our life. It is Jesus who brings us back to reality. His words remind us that the pathway to peace and joy is found in Him. That pathway is a person. It is our close walk with Him that pushes the darkness away. *"Again Jesus spoke to them, saying, "I am the light of the world. Whoever follows me will not walk in darkness, but will have the light of life.""* (John 8:12)

As we follow King Jesus through Death's Shadow Valley, we do not walk in darkness. We will have the light of the life of God to guide us. Turning page after page, reading word after word out loud, God ministered to my soul in ways I cannot even fathom yet today. Doubt and worry were removed. Fear and loss were comforted. Anxiety and panic were done away with.

In their place was King Jesus. He was there in my room, alongside of me, and in the car as I drove to my appointments. I'm not sure when it happened, but one day I realize that while I was alone I wasn't anymore. His presence was with me. I knew that was true because of His peace.

I had found these words from the apostle Paul to be true in the midst of my broken heart. I had chosen *"not be anxious about anything, but in everything by prayer and supplication with thanksgiving let your requests be made known to God."* And I had found that, *"the peace of God, which surpasses all understanding, will guard your hearts and your minds in Christ Jesus."* (Philippians 4:6–7)

That's what I had: The peace of God! I couldn't understand it. I couldn't explain it. Yet my heart and my mind were at rest. No, I was not happy with Melodee being gone. It was not what I wanted. But I knew, somehow, that God was with me and he was leading me into the next season of my life. He was making the rest of my life the best of my life. And that made no sense at all to me. However I trusted the One who was leading me. Will you do that today?

Presence for Our Confusion. Some believe that the death of their loved one is a direct result of some failure on their part. But God isn't that kind of person. He reminds us of His presence in our lives in every horrible situation by telling us *"Be strong and courageous. Do not fear or be in dread of them, for it is the LORD your God who goes with you. He will not leave you or forsake you"* (Deuteronomy 31:6) and then He reaffirms that truth in the New Testament when He says it again, *"I will never leave you nor forsake you."* (Hebrews 13:5)

The peace of God comes from the presence of God in our midst. In my pain I always had a choice. My choice was simple: Do I invite Jesus in to my life at this point of pain and confusion and sorrow? Or, do I reject Jesus because He did not answer my prayers for the healing of Melodee that I prayed and believed Him for? If that's the place you are right now, then what will you do? God wants to offer us His presence and thus His peace. We must trust God when it makes no sense at all. That is what faith is all about. And I am here to tell you it is so, so worth it.

Stability for Our Imbalance. When Melodee died nothing seemed right. The holidays were upon me. Thanksgiving, Christmas, New Year's, Valentine's Day… all without the one I had forged life's story with. How could I navigate without my navigator? How could I enjoy without my partner?

Melodee had always bought all the presents for all the people in our lives. She was a master at planning. Months before of birthday or a holiday she already had the gift and it was wrapped and labeled! Now, here I was, days away from Christmas with little desire to be a part of any festivities, much less bring gifts.

Yet as the New Year started to unfold, the courage and strength of the Holy Spirit began to flow in and through me once more. I began to sense God had a greater purpose for me. In all of this, God began to reveal to me that He was answering prayers that I had prayed over the past *decades*.

When I began to ask him for clarity, He provided it through His words, which I read each morning, with certainty. God did have a plan. I wasn't off track. God was leading me. I just needed to trust Him more. And through those times alone with God He melted my loneliness, He was healing my soul, and He was building me into the man He wanted me to become for the purposes He had designed me for in this season of my life.

You may be struggling with Your situation, and the pain of being alone may seem too much right now. I want to encourage you to get alone with God every day. Opens His words and read them out loud. And as your faith becomes greater every day, you too will experience the melting of your loneliness as His presence fills your heart and mind and soul through Jesus our King.

Why not use the Bible reading schedule at the end of this book right now? Even if you jump in to the midst of a story or a situation in a Bible book that you have no idea what's going on in, just start reading. And before you read ask God to speak to you through the pages of His words and bring healing to your loneliness.

It has been my experience as I've walked through Death's Shadow Valley, that God and God alone can heal our loneliness and restore our happiness. I encourage you trust God in this. He has a pathway out of darkness and into the light. And He wants to share it with you... one day at a time, one step at a time, one healing at a time. Today is a great day to start removing your loneliness.

Taking Action

Consider: It is our close walk with King Jesus that pushes the darkness of loneliness away.

Trust: *"I am the light of the world. Whoever follows me will not walk in darkness, but will have the light of life."* (John 8:12)

Act: *Get alone with God every day. Open His words and read them out loud and ask God to speak to you through the pages of His words and bring healing to your loneliness.*

8
Reminders

Melting Under the Glimpse of Their Presence

"Blessed are those who mourn, for they shall be comforted." (Matthew 5:4)

Every morning, as I go to the refrigerator, I see the post-it written in Melodee's hand, "For Marisa. Love, Melodee." Melodee gave it to Marisa with the hanging hand towel she had made as a gift before she was promoted.

While most of the time I look at it with fondness, sometimes – mind you just sometimes – her distinctive handwriting and the fact that there will be no more such notes brings me to tears.

You see, every time I went on a trip anywhere with an overnight bag or a suitcase, every piece of clothing had a note expressing her deep love for me. Some were affectionate, some were romantic, some were encouraging, some were with longing for my return, and some were… well, let's just say they reminded me why I shouldn't be gone too long!

And now, each day, I see her hand on that note and I miss her love, her affection, her belief in me – her Captain America! When I'm feeling stronger, it brings me joy. And when I'm feeler weaker, it brings me to tears.

Reminders Are Everywhere

The good, the bad, and the ugly of grief is that there are reminders are everywhere. I know some people try to eradicate them as fast as they can by giving everything of their loved ones' away. But that is impossible because your restaurant, your grocery store, your church, your favorite places can't be razed. They will always be there. They will remind me of her… and that's not a bad thing. *I don't want to forget her.* I just want to remember her without so much pain.

Others go to the opposite extreme – they keep everything in place like a shrine. I once heard a story of someone who left her husband's dirty clothes laid out the way he had left them – for years. This is unhealthy. Unless our loved one was obsessional and selfish, they wouldn't want us to be frozen in a moment. They would want us to live the rest of our lives as the best of our lives.

When going through Melodee's things after her promotion I ran across so many things that caused the grief to flow. I found the handmade Father's Day card she made for me – the last Father's Day card – she was in the hospital that day. The front of the folded piece of paper read, *"This Father's Day there's no fancy store bought card, no steak dinner, no pampering like you deserve… but… "*. And then, on the inside she wrote, *"It doesn't mean that I don't think you deserve all those things and more! It just means once again you're my super hero and you're busy doing super hero stuff for me! Happy Father's Day! Love, hugs and kisses! MJ"* On the back she had drawn Cap's shield and then wrote these words, "My Hero!"

Imagine the tears that flowed like faucets when I reread that card! However, because it shows the deep love of Melodee's heart, despite the pain and sickness she was experiencing, that card has a prominent place in my bedroom where I can see it all the time. Around my room you will also find some of the poster size pictures from her Memorial Service. There's the collage of photos put together by her niece, Robin. Then there's my favorite picture of the four of us together for Tabitha's wedding. And Melodee's favorite picture, taken after she was diagnosed and in pain, of her and the four granddaughters – including the newly-minted Sianna – sitting in a rocking chair smiles ablaze.

Every trip to the bedroom reminds me of her passionate love for me, for the girls, for the grands, for her family. And, you see, I *want* to remember that. Despite the pain and the ache it creates, which lessens with each passing week, with exceptions of course as I mentioned in chapter 6, I *want* to remember the good times. I *want* to relive the laughter and joy. I *don't* want to forget.

Having said all that I *choose* to move forward because God has brought me to *this place* in my life not to stay stuck on November 11, 2017, not to stay stuck at 38 years, 5 months, and 2 days, but to move into the next season of my life. Why? Because *whatever* God does is right. I can trust Him today to move me forward just as I've trusted Him in the past. Through every storm God has been there because God is with me. And He is with you, right now.

The question is: will we *choose* to move forward so the rest of our lives can be the best of our lives? If we aren't dead ourselves, then we aren't done! God's will isn't finished with us. So, every day I fall on my knees, surrender afresh and ask God, "What do you want me to do today?" Let me encourage you to pray that prayer. Let me encourage you to move forward, starting right now.

Moving Forward

So, what does it take to move forward *with* all the reminders that come across our path? Understanding that moving forward is a process was essential to my healing. As I started moving forward I discovered some things that have helped immensely.

Understand it will be painful. Grief is painful. Period. We can't sugar coat it and we can't live in denial. We've been deeply torn. We have a gaping, bleeding wound that many have no experiential frame of reference to understand us by. However, we have to stop, drop, and roll each time the pain flows from our emotional and psychological roundedness. We have to stop and admit to ourselves and to others that we are wounded and in need of healing.

Once we do that, we can drop to our knees and humbly admit our weakness to God. Perhaps the most surprising part for me was realizing that I needed healing. When Marisa told me one day, "Pastor Matt, we just want to be a place of healing for you." I realized I was in denial. I *hadn't even thought* I needed healing. Now, on my knees each night, I ask God to heal me. In my prayer time each morning, I ask God to heal my torn and wounded heart.

That's the healing step. Rolling all my ache and pain onto the Lord, I tell him everything. From the hurt of missing Melodee to the pain of wanting a new wife whom I can adore and who will adore me, I share it all with Him. I simply pour out my pain and my complaints and tell Him how I know the process is important but I HATE the process. I just want to be well. I want to be married. I want to be loved. I want to be held. I want to be reconnected again (see chapter 5). I want someone to believe in me again – as her Captain America!

Choose to enjoy the pain. I know, that sounds wrong! Hear me out. I think I can convince you it is right, even if it doesn't sound like it right now. Grief creates pain. Pain comes from loss. Loss comes from love. We only grieve the ones we love. The greater the grief we experience, the greater the love we have had for them. So, If we start thinking, *Grief = Love*, we'll start reversing the damage of grief, turning it into healing.

That is what I had forgotten on that first Resurrection Day I mentioned in chapter 6. Instead of focusing on the love and joy, the fun and friendship I had with Melodee and allowing the joy-filled videos to play in my heart, all I could do was be selfish and sulk. And that was, and is, unhealthy and destructive.

Embrace the love that grief invokes. Choosing to replay Melodee's love for me, remembering her constant care of me, embracing her compassion to me when I failed or hurt, drawing on her intense belief in me (remember, she called me *"her hero," "her Captain America"*) changes who I am today and what I will become tomorrow. And that is how God heals my heart and yours. The video we replay in our minds will determine our mental, emotional, and physical health in the months and years to come.

What we feed our souls determines our spiritual health just as much as what we feed our bodies determines our physical health. What are you feeding your soul? Are you waddling in self-pity? Or, are you swimming in their love? It's a daily – often hourly – choice. But make no mistake it is a choice we have to make ourselves.

Ask friends to pray. While this seems like a "no brainer" to most, we often mistake the fact that we *have* asked people for their prayers in the past with the reality that we must *ask people again* for their prayers today; especially at the moment of our new grief. Many don't like to be so transparent and would rather "suffer in silence." Yet, as I have shared before, and I will share again, there is NOTHING godly about becoming a hermit and disconnecting. Choose to call, text, or email immediately when the cloud of darkness moves in. God answers the prayers of the righteous.

Draw caring people alongside. There are a few very close friends whom I reach out to immediately. They know me well and know how to speak life into me. I depend on them in crisis times when I am being swallowed alive in the vortex of pain and darkness.

Choosing those people carefully is essential. Sliding into the abyss is no time to have an insensitive "friend" tell you to "Get over it!" or "Are you *still* grieving?" My inner circle of "go to," people know that when I contact them, I need them now. Whether that is to pray, to talk or to put a hand on my shoulder and just let me cry it out.

Focus on God's will for our future. My goal in this season is to "walk THROUGH the Valley of the Shadow of Death." I don't want to camp here and I'm surely not building my home here. I'm heading to the mountain because *"goodness and mercy shall follow me all the days of my life."* (Psalm 23:6)

Thus, each night I surrender afresh to God's path, His plan, and His desires for my life. You see, I have LIFE! And Jesus promised that I *"may have life and have it abundantly."* (John 10:10) So, with each new sunrise I know that two messengers of God are chasing me down: Goodness and Mercy. I want to slow my pace each day and deliberately look for them, like one looks out the window for the pizza deliveryman. When they catch me, I will savor their gifts like hot cheese and pepperoni on that pie!

That's the life I am focused on. Not the one locked in the funeral home, but the one free and rejoicing over God's plan. The questions today are: Do you believe God is good? Do you believe God is *still* good, even after the death of your loved one? Do you believe that *whatever* God does is right? Are you looking for God's two agents of the abundant life today: Goodness and Mercy?

Faith is about seeing the unseen. *"Now faith is the reality of what is hoped for, the proof of what is not seen."* (Hebrews 11:1, CSB) Are we walking in faith or are we walking in doubt. That's the point of reminders. They remind us that God is good. They remind us that God is kind. They remind us that He will be *again.* And we have to trust Him and His character and tell Him afresh today, "This plan sucks, but I am surrendered because I trust You. What do you want me to do next Lord, so the rest of my life can be the best of my life?" God will answer and you will have hope again!

Taking Action

Consider: Do you believe God is *still* good, even after the death of your loved one?

Trust: *"Goodness and mercy shall follow me all the days of my life."* (Psalm 23:6)

Act: Tell God afresh today, "This plan sucks, but I am surrendered because I trust You. What do you want me to do next Lord, so the rest of my life can be the best of my life?"

9
Relatives

Living with The Good, The Bad, and The Ugly

"Let no one seek his own good, but the good of his neighbor."
(1 Corinthians 10:24)

Someone has rightly said, "We can pick our friends but we're stuck with our relatives!" Nothing seems to magnify the character of a relative more than death. Having been in the funeral home too often to count with my family, I am all too familiar with how relatives respond to the death of their "loved one."

Yet, when it comes to the death of our loved one, our spouse, we are hoping that our family will be our best refuge and support in the midst of this walk through Death's Shadow Valley. From most of our relatives that will be true. But for others, well, perhaps only or a few or one, their character will be revealed most clearly at this most inopportune time.

Melodee's departure for Heaven was predicated on the short return of that dreaded monster: Cancer. At the beginning it seems like everything and everyone within the family were in agreement. And that was a huge help.

Knowing the sensitive nature of this discussion and the personal aspects of it, I want to speak in specific generalities as much as possible. While the illustrations would be more potent if more details were shared, I know that you will get the basic gist of what I'm talking about without me having to name names or give details that would reveal specific individual's names.

At this moment I want to say plainly, that in virtually every situation where someone's life partner has died, someone in the family will bite like a viper, they will wound like a bear. But for every malcontent and mischievous soul inside our family tree, we can rest assured that most of us will be surrounded by an abundance of helpers, lovers, and pray-ers. And in their love, we will experience their *"Love one another with brotherly affection. Outdo one another in showing honor."* (Romans 12:10)

So let's talk a little bit about relatives as we walk through the Valley of the Shadow of Death.

In-laws, Outlaws, and Other Kinds of Relatives

Struggling to tell the girls the Melodee had been promoted was one of the most difficult things I have ever done in my life. Both of them were rushing to get back to see their mother one last time. Tabitha was sitting alone in a London airport waiting for her flight when I called. Hannah had stopped for the night just waiting for the sun to rise and make the last part of the 1400-mile drive.

Fearing I would miss Tabitha as she boarded her plane I called her. My pain and grief was overwhelming. And to tell her that she was not going to see her mother again this side of Heaven was beyond heartbreaking. With tears streaming down my face, convulsing while I talked, I shared the news knowing that Tabitha would have to fly over 15 hours from London to Los Angeles before she would get to me.

Then, the call to Hannah. She knew things were not good just because I called so early in the morning. It must've been 3:30 a.m. when I told her the awful news. She had driven so far in one day – from Waco, Texas to Phoenix, Arizona – with four children, and pregnant. Now she would make the last of the trip without any more sleep, having to take the children out of their beds, only to explain to them their grandma was in Heaven.

It is at these moments that we need our family. Knowing Hannah would be with me in a few hours and Tabitha would be with me by the end of the day brought great comfort in the midst of the greatest pain I've ever felt in my entire life.

In the meantime, while I waited for their arrival, my LA family – Pastor Bryan, Marisa, and Micah – held me, wept with me, loved on me, and supported me. Without them at that moment I would have collapsed as the funeral home came and took Melodee's earthly tent away.

Looking Backwards Now, Wondering

Those next days with Tabitha and Hannah, Michael, and our granddaughters were amazing. Since Melodee was promoted on November 11, just two weeks before Thanksgiving in the United States, we enjoyed time together until Tabitha flew home just before the holiday. Hannah, Michael, and the girls then drove back to Texas the day after Thanksgiving. It was so good to be together in such an awful time.

Looking backwards now, I'm surprised by some of the relative's responses. I want to be selective in my comments, but I want to be real so you understand what to expect. These are my experiences and I hope that yours are better than some of mine.

Some relatives will think only of you. When your family is as spread out as ours was at the time of Melodee's home going, you realize that it's difficult for everyone to come along side of you at the initial moment of your need. Yet, you've probably discovered that you don't really want everybody traipsing through your bleeding heart at that particular moment. Sometimes you just need to be alone in the quiet and cry.

Yet, we all need the support and love of our family at such a time as this. Even though they were far away, some of the relatives made sure that they called and messaged expressing their desire to help in any way possible. Missing a call or two along the way, some of the relatives left the most amazing, beautiful, grace filled words of support I've ever heard.

From across the country those loved ones checked in and supported at just the right time. I can remember one of the calls particularly well. I played and played it, over and over again. Those words of love and tenderness from one of Melodee's family members still touch me to this day.

During those first hours and days, and in the weeks ahead through the holidays of Thanksgiving and Christmas and New Year's, loved ones came along side me, set messages, continued to call and to express their love and prayers.

Since the memorial service for Melodee would be held after New Year's in January as per her orders before she was promoted, those two months were filled with opportunities to express love and care and concern. Small gifts, cards, cash, checks, and words of compassion lifted my heart and seem to arrive just in time when the darkness of grief wanted to take hold again.

Some relatives will think only of themselves. As much as some relatives can literally pull you out the pit of despair others seem to be more concerned with their own personal feelings even though it's *you* who lost your life partner. If you're honest, and you have gone through this Dark Valley of Death already, you have found some relatives that very early on showed their hand of selfishness.

Character cannot be covered up for very long. Soon the reality of self-centeredness will rear its ugly head and expect that everyone – including you – make *them* the center of everything.

I am sorry if you experience this. My prayer is that you never have to. Yet the reality is that some people are more concerned with their own feelings, their own lifestyle, and their own schedule than they will ever be about you, your pain, and your loss.

Though I cannot share specific illustrations here because they would immediately be telling and those closest to the family would have no question as to whom I'm speaking of, let me simply conclude this thought by saying that if your loved one was not taken suddenly, clues were already there for you to prepare your heart.

Selfish people tolerate others. Even when things are bad, as in Melodee's case with her cancer, even our relatives won't be able to cover up the inconvenience that your spouse is creating in their lives. Again my prayer is you never have to experience this pain for it is like someone stepping on your broken arm. And the scars from that pain take a lot longer to heal that even the scars from the death of our spouse.

Dealing with (and Healing From) the Relatives

Let me say that at the beginning of our experience of pain and grief, our loved ones are expected to lift us up, to carry us, and take care of us. We need not say much in appreciation except, "Thank you." They understand and we should understand that we are not there to help them or to care for them. Everything is quite the opposite.

Love on the Loving

As the days turn into weeks and the weeks turn into months, it is totally appropriate to not only express our gratitude in cards and calls, but if we are able to actually entertain them we can do so with perhaps a meal out or over coffee. This is part of the healing process. We are becoming human again after being shredded by death.

So think about how you might say, "Thank you!" to that relative whose love touched your life. I always like to go the extra mile when possible. And so a nice meal out, a time when I can express my great gratitude, and some sacrifice on my part will express my love for them quite nicely.

At Thanksgiving we all pitched in and I made the turkey! Yes, it is one of my trademark dishes. You see, loving on those relatives who are so helpful in these awful days is just part of walking out from Death's Shadow Valley.

Dealing with the Selfish

In her lifetime on Earth, Melodee was the Great Reconciler. Whether it was a strained relationship at church or within our family, Melodee would wade neck-deep into the mess and almost always bring about unity and harmony. She was brave and fearless and prayer filled.

She believed, "Blessed are the peacemakers." (Matthew 5:9) And so, what struck me as so very odd was when she gave up on one of the relatives. It was totally out of her character. I could have blamed the cancer, the drugs, or the pain for such a response. But I choose to tell you that since I knew her so well I believe she had simply gotten to the end of her belief.

The "end of her belief," you ask? Yes. *The end of her belief.* She simply had come to a place where she realized that the selfishness that inhabited this relative could not be expunged in what remained of her lifetime. And so she simply walked away.

Now if we were dealing with me, and we were telling my story, and this is how it had developed there would be a totally different cause. However, Melodee was using all of her energy to bring about healing. As cancer was eating its way through her body she had to spend her time resting and taking care of herself.

While she remained a great prayer warrior, she simply decided with this relative to step back and only pray. It wasn't that she didn't love anymore. It was that she did not have the energy to bring about an understanding in this relative's heart. She was fighting for her life. And so she prayed and left the self-centered relative in God's hands.

We are to love our enemies. This is perhaps one of the most difficult commands of Jesus for those of us who tend to have issues with the people who wound us. If your relatives have injured you during this time you know the difficulty of loving those people. If I could get you to be honest with me, I would say that there was probably a long-term pattern of being repeatedly wounded by this very same relative long before death ever visited your house.

Jesus calls us to deal with those who hurt us in the following way: *"I say to you, Love your enemies and pray for those who persecute you, so that you may be sons of your Father who is in heaven."* (Matthew 5:44–45)

Love them. For the bad and the ugly relatives who wound us in the midst of our grief and pain we are called to love. We aren't called to spend a lot of time with them at this point in our lives. Our main priority is to heal from our sorrow. Returning to the scene of the crime can be asking for more pain and suffering.

Like the father in the prodigal son story, we can love someone without chasing them down and bringing them to their senses. It was the father who waited for the son to return before reconciliation could happen. As Jesus tells the story, we read these words: *"But when he came to himself... he arose and came to his father. But while he was still a long way off, his father saw him and felt compassion, and ran and embraced him and kissed him."* (Luke 15:17, 20)

Pray for them. For now just love them and pray for them. You probably were already praying for this person anyway. After all, selfish people don't just all of a sudden manifest their selfishness at times of death. At family gatherings it's all about them. They don't mind having their own way even when it hurts you or others. And so, if you are walking with Jesus, you have probably already prayed for them. Just keep praying for them.

Apart from the work of God selfish people do not change. Change comes when they come to their senses. They change when God transforms their heart and brings them to surrender. So today, pray for them. Tomorrow, or some tomorrow in the future, there might even be a time for reconciliation. Today, trust God to work in answer to your prayers. And remember he sees your pain and how they're treating you or ignoring you. Just make your healing your number one priority. God will deal with our selfish relatives in His own way and on His schedule.

Taking Action

Consider: Doing life in the light is what not only keeps grief at bay but brings life, healing and wholeness.

Trust: *"I came that they may have life and have it abundantly."* (John 10:10)

Act: *Lord, how do I make the rest of my life the best of my life?*

10

Bad Advice

Silencing the Voices That Want To Control You

"As for you, you whitewash with lies; worthless physicians are you all."
(Job 13:4)

"You should wait a year before you even *consider* looking for a new mate." Time and time again one of my close *married* friends would begin to tell me how I should proceed, how I should *feel,* how long I should wait… honestly, you know how this goes. People who have <u>never</u> experienced our pain and its months, or years, of loneliness act as Job's counselors!

Now, to be fair, most all of them mean well. But, really, some of their counsel has inflicted more hurt than I thought I could bear. Others, after sharing their folly, can't seem to understand why I'm upset with their words. Seriously? Are you considering who I am and who Melodee was? Are you comparing me to your acquaintance that is totally unlike us? Am I *really* that irresponsible? Did you *not* listen to my carefully thought out plan?

Yes, your friend ran off the deep end. I understand they came back with a far less than desirable partner because they were lonely. Sure, they made a bad choice because of their pain and tried to slather it with someone – anyone – who would anesthetize the pain.

However, I'm not just *anyone,* and neither are you, since you picked up this book. My relationship with Melodee was transparent, open, honest, and clear. We talked about this subject in detail. There was no confusion about her hopes and dreams for me, just as there were none about mine for her.

And it happened again – this week. Another person was trying to tell me what MY wife of 38 years, five months and two days meant by her words.

A Frequent Occurrence

It was Wednesday afternoon, the week before she was promoted to Heaven at 3:05 am Saturday morning, when she leaned forward in her hospital bed and said, "You. Will. Get. Married. Again." Then she sat back and finished her counsel. "Wait one year."

We had been talking about this subject since she brought it up the first time, 10 years before at the first occurrence of her endometrial cancer. I *knew full well* what she meant. We had watched her father, Bill, marry within three months barely knowing the woman and wreck a lifetime's reputation in the process.

There, in her hospital room, as we discussed options and possibilities, Melodee's words were clear and well understood: "Give it some time and don't make my dad's mistake! I trust you. You will know who it is once you develop a close friendship, like you did with me. You're going to marry your best friend, so take the year to get to know someone really well if you think you want to marry them."

Melodee and I often relied on a simple truth, a promise as deep as the heart of God itself: "*Delight yourself in the L\ord, and he will give you the desires of your heart.*" (Psalm 37:4) God longs to bring joy to our wounded souls. That joy always finds its source in Him. And, when we are close to the Lord, He will provide all we need to live the life we desire, even after the death of our spouse.

Over a decade – since the first occurrence of her cancer – we had talked these things through. We made our intentions clear. We spoke life into those plans. We counseled each other on our plans. We laughed and challenged each other about specifics in those plans for our futures without each other... *that* was who we were. *That* is where this strategy is coming from. *That* is the security I have... a decade of honest dealing with this now all-too-real scenario of being a widower.

Dealing with Bad Advice

Over the course of the first months of my new status as a single man, I discovered that my faith in God and my clarity about my future direction – both born out of an intimate and consistent time alone with God have provided some wisdom in dealing with my less than helpful self-appointed counselors.

Be patient. First and foremost, I have to remember that the person giving me their thoughts cares for me. After all, they wouldn't have gotten this close to bring up the subject if I hadn't let them in. So, I have learned that, while they may not have a clue what they are talking about, they do *love* me.

64

Be gracious. Some of the counsel is simply, to be honest, awful! Based on their culture or their opinion, they simply blurt out what they think without thinking about my heart and feelings. While I am bleeding and in more pain because of their insensitivity to where I'm at, I remember that *we are still* children of the Most High God and there is no excuse for being rude. Choose to be filled with grace, despite the counsel you receive.

Be attentive. One of the surprising realities that I've come to realize is that God often speaks to me *through* their bad counselor! No, I am not saying their words are correct. However, often the ideas they bring up are used by the Spirit of God to direct me to issues that I may not have given any or enough thought about. So listen carefully to the Spirit of God even when the advice is bad.

Be honest. One of the hardest things I had to do early on was to tell a dearly loved friend they were absolutely wrong. I found myself saying to them, "Did you *ever* really know my wife?" With their attention fully engaged on my heart and words, I explained the frank and honest decade of discussion we had over this subject. As I graciously revealed the reality, as opposed to their fantasy, they slowly and reluctantly let go of their preconceived and ill-advised counsel.

Be direct. There is nothing wrong with being honest and blunt when it is done with grace and mercy. Telling someone the truth, in love, is what we are called to do (See Ephesians 4:15). I have found that countering the bad advice at the end of a lengthy discussion doesn't help much. It is easier to jump in earlier and steer the discussion. Showing our confused friend or loved one the error of their assumptions with specifics often moves them to relent or repent of their position.

Be gone. And then, there are some who, simply think they are right and we are wrong unless we live our lives according to their counsel. And what can we do with that? Simply thank them for their ideas and get up and leave.

It does us no good to listen and grow angry. Neither is it helpful to sit there and cause them to assume they are correct – after all, they will inflict more of their foolishness on another bleeding man or woman.

While you don't have to be dramatic, I simply and politely excuse myself with an explanation often something like this. "Well, had you truly known

Melodee, you would understand where I am coming from. Thanks for caring. Blessings!" And then I get up and leave.

You Can't Avoid Bad Advice

Let's be honest. It's *your* life. How you live it will *always* invite criticism and unsolicited counsel. The difference now is that we are vulnerable and people know they can get away with saying things to us they would never be able to normally because we are hurting.

They expect that we will sit there and take their counsel as if delivered from the Lord Jesus himself. That is not a script I am willing to work from, and it shouldn't be for you as well.

God is directing our lives, and He has been since long before we were conceived. We live and die for Him. And, in this season, when we feel like we are doing both at the same time, we must follow His counsel, counsel hammered out in the long hours before His face with His words open before us.

As my friend and fellow traveler through Death's Shadow Valley said to me often, "You will make it through this. You have come so far. It will be okay again." THAT is the counsel you need and that is the type of counselor we all need to listen to. Find that person and allow them to speak life into your healing soul.

Taking Action

Consider: God is directing our lives, and He has been since long before we were conceived. We live and die for Him.

Trust: *"Delight yourself in the LORD, and he will give you the desires of your heart."* (Psalm 37:4)

Act: Follow God's counsel, counsel hammered out in the long hours before His face with His words open before us.

11

Expectations

Adjusting Our Fantasies with Our Reality

"For God alone, O my soul, wait in silence, for my hope is from him. He only is my rock and my salvation, my fortress; I shall not be shaken." (Psalm 62:5–6)

Let's face it. Life will never go back to normal, at least a normal that we used to have with our spouse. That's just reality. And as much as we want them back, they aren't coming back. And so one of our fantasies has to meet reality right away. They aren't coming back. And we have to go on. Fantasy versus reality.

So how do we go on? We have to deal with this world of hurt. When I wake up in the morning I realize she's not beside me. When I go to bed at night she's not there. There's no one to call or text or message. Reality simply hurts at this moment in our lives.

You're probably thinking that you wish your life wasn't the way it is. I understand and I am sorry. I wish it wasn't this way also. But all the wishing that we might put in will not change the reality that God has brought to us. We are going to have to deal with the life we have, not the life we had.

What a Mess!

Depending on where you are in this journey through the Valley of the Shadow of Death, you may have recently realized you are all alone. I mean we knew that almost immediately. When Melodee breathed her last breath I felt it. Emotionally, psychologically, spiritually, and physically I felt her leave.

That's not what I mean. Despite all of the pain and the agony and the sorrow then, there was somebody around us almost the entire time in those early days afterward. Whether it was close friends or family, we could depend on somebody, anybody, to help. Whether it was to bring us some food, get us a glass of water, run an errand, or just sit with us so we weren't so alone, there was somebody there. Now we've come to realize things are *different*.

People go back to their lives. Whether it's through my personal experience now or my experience as a pastor, one cold hard truth comes to bear: *Life goes on.* The cruel reality is that life goes on... whether we like it or not. There's work and children and mortgage payments and church events and life. They all cry out to those who were so helpful to us during those initially brutal days.

Now we find ourselves hearing the clock tick. We notice the breeze that blows. We wonder if that car engine we hear is someone coming to see us. And when will all those promises be fulfilled? You know the ones I mean. "If you need anything just call." "We're here if you need us." "We'll have you over for dinner real soon." And yet another day comes and goes and no one calls or asks us over to eat. People go back to their lives and while they might have a thought or two about us, the cares of their world pull them very strongly.

Family has to get on with their life. We probably understand when our friends are busy. What might be far more difficult for us is when our family doesn't come by. We've grown accustomed to supporting one another as family and when they don't come by or help, let's face it, it hurts. Again though, the reality is that our family has to get on with their life too.

Loneliness can eat away one's soul if we allow it to. In fact, we can tell the acid of loneliness has begun to destroy us when we feel a bitter resentment over members of our family who seemingly have forgotten about us. We have to fight that. We have to realize that pain magnifies. And at this moment, as everyone is going back to their own worlds, we will have to understand and be patient and start reforming our own world.

Friends don't know what to do with us anymore. One of the things that I came to realize was that our friends were mostly all couples. So when we did things, Melodee and I made a foursome. Now I was no longer a couple. As a single man, I didn't make any couple a foursome anymore. And when I did go out with those couples it felt… different. Let's be honest, it *was* different.

Melodee and I were a team, a partnership, a couple. We would finish each other's lines, interpret what each other was saying, add funny parts to the stories the other one missed telling, and in general depended on each other to carry a conversation when we were together with our friends. Now all of that was gone. And friends noticed it. What's more, some of them didn't know what to do with it. Thank God that wasn't everybody!

Life grows so much more difficult. And every day, with growing frequency, it became apparent that life was growing more and more difficult. True, there was only one of us now to make dishes and clothes dirty. And equally true was that there was also only one of us wash them, fold them (in the case of the laundry – not the dishes), and put them away. It seemed that each week things begin to pile up more and more even as I worked to remove them.

Finances and recording paid bills have never been my strong suit. Melodee would always pay the bills, organize the files, and make sure that things were ready for the taxman. My crash course at her bedside before her promotion to Heaven for 20 or 30 minutes was surely not enough to help me with this lingering problem. And it takes so much time! While I'm trying to do everything else, this has to be done also.

How Do We Cope?

By now you're beginning to understand, unless you've been at this for a while as a single person, that our expectations that things will go on smoothly don't come to pass. The reality is the things get more and more difficult. Is there a way to get a handle on all of this? Are there any understandings that can help run our reality? Let me share just a few ideas on what I did with the reality that we now live in versus the expectations that we may have had.

Stop trying to do it all. The reality is one person cannot do all the things that two people have done. It took me a while to come to this conclusion. Add to that all that needs to be done now because our life partner has been departed and we come up with a huge issue: All my work + all of her work + all of this new work = too much work!

Focus on what's essential. You can't do it all! So stop trying! In every season there are priorities. Remember that your first priority is always to get well, to heal. In the early days after Melodee's departure I had to deal with all of the attendant financial issues. Sometimes it was overwhelming. At times the forms and the procedures overwhelmed me. And then, from time to time, I was overwhelmed by my grief as I filled out or did that procedure or form.

One day I simply did what I am very good at, I made a plan. I said to myself, "What do I have to do *this* week?" I made a list and then that was about all I did that week as far as projects went. I made sure that those two or three vital issues got taken care of (well, most of the time).

In the early days you will not have the strength to do what you used to do. And that's okay. You will probably put too many things on your to-do list in the early days, so prioritize them. What must you do first? Second? Third? If you put four or five things on your list, and you only get three of them done, you'll want to make sure that the things that have due dates on them are at the top of your to do list in priority.

You will be amazed at how much peace comes to us when we do things in a manner that gets rid of the urgent things on our to do list first. Of course there are many, many things that we have to do, mundane things. As I said earlier, dishes need to be washed and so do clothes. You'll have to take time to cry and some days you will not have the strength to get out of bed too early because you haven't slept much the night before.

So don't put too much on your calendar each day and make sure that the things that are there cover the most urgent first. It will breathe health and strength and hope into your soul when the urgent gets taken care of.

Indulge yourself some. You may have been surprised when you read those words, *"indulge yourself some."* Balancing our expectations with reality is a matter of putting some of our expectations into our reality. Just because everything is falling apart doesn't mean that it has to stay that way.

I happen to love frozen yogurt. Los Angeles County is filled with many places for me to have my indulgence. And so, after a particularly difficult day or set of days, I would find myself having some frozen yogurt. Often I would invite a friend to come along but then again, I could simply just stop *anytime* I wanted to because I was driving by and I would sit there and have a cup of frozen yogurt (with lots of maraschino cherries on top, of course!).

Life goes on. It's not like I ate buckets and buckets of frozen yogurt, thus getting as big as a beach ball in weight and size. Yet my occasional frozen yogurt cup was a delightful treat in the midst of those difficult days. Adding good friends to the mix simply made it sweeter. And I want to remind you again that our primary mission during our times of grief is to heal. Your small indulgences help you heal more quickly (but don't get fat as a result).

Follow God's leading. One of the most amazing things in this process came out of my personal time alone with the Lord. As we've talked about time and again, because it's so much a part of who I am, those times alone with God are times to listen to His voice through His words in the Bible and then listen to the Spirit's voice as He seeks to apply what I've read to what God's doing with me.

So imagine early on when God began to prompt me to travel around the United States. In fact, if I was honest with you right now, the whole idea came almost in one moment. While all of the details did not crystallize for weeks, the general structure of the trip, even when to go, fell into place through the leading of God's Spirit.

I love to travel. I have wanderlust. One of the most favorite things that Melodee and I would do was to travel and to explore. But the size of this trip was a little daunting even for myself. But in the days and weeks ahead as God and I spoke about this trip it became crystal clear that this was His will.

And so as I planned and contacted friends with whom I would stay with along the way. Even when plans fell apart, God sent me a backup friend and plan! That trip was the defining moment of my healing. For 12 weeks over 23 states in 27 cities driving 9,608 miles, God work miracles in my soul.

I would like to tell you that it was a constant joy. The reality is that I had some great heartache and pain that walked me through some preconceived notions, some expectations that never materialized, and some sorrows I had not healed from. However, by the time I had returned to Los Angeles, I was a different man because I had followed the leading of God. Today I'm so very grateful, and forever will be, for following the leading of God on this matter.

Have some fun! When we put the words at grief and fun together someone's going to be upset. And all I can say is, you haven't healed yet. The second fruit of the Holy Spirit, according to Paul in Galatians chapter 5 is joy! *"But the fruit of the Spirit is love, JOY, peace, patience, kindness, goodness, faithfulness, gentleness, self-control."* (Galatians 5:22–23)

God created fun so that He could bring health and healing into our soul. God wants joy to spill out like a river from our innermost being. He's planned it that way. And today God is saying to you that He wants you to have some fun. Now what you do for fun and what I do for fun are probably very different. As long as it's moral and pleasing in God sight, go do it!

Some will never understand that you're having fun while you're grieving. The critically religious never do. Jesus had to deal with them in His day. Moses had to deal with them. We all have to deal with the critically religious, but we do not have to listen to them. It's good for you to laugh. Listen to the words of the wisest man in the Old Testament: *"A joyful heart is good medicine, but a crushed spirit dries up the bones."* (Proverbs 17:22)

I'm not sure which you would rather be – joyful or crushed – but I choose to be joyful! After all, the critically religious sound like the second half of that proverb, don't they? In fact why don't you do yourself a favor right now? Take a moment and write down the three things you like to do most that bring fun of your life. Here I've even given you a place to write them down…

    1. _______________________________________

    2. _______________________________________

    3. _______________________________________

Did you get them written down? Is there one of them you can do this week? Do you need someone to do it with you? Why not to call them up right now and ask them if they would join you? You'll be so surprised at how you will feel after you make that phone call or send that text message. Imagine how much better you're going to feel after you go do that thing you enjoy so much!

Your life is all about getting well. Your expectations shatter that process. Once we pick up the pieces of our broken hopes, we realize that in the midst of our dark reality we can begin to shine the light of Jesus Christ and find healing, strength, and yes, even hope to help in this most terrible time in our lives.

Taking Action

Consider: Just because everything is falling apart doesn't mean that it has to stay that way.

Trust: *"A joyful heart is good medicine, but a crushed spirit dries up the bones."* (Proverbs 17:22)

Act: Today God is saying to you that He wants you to have some fun, so as long as it's moral and pleasing in God sight, go do it!

12

Help

Learning to Accept What Others Have to Offer

"Two are better than one, because they have a good reward for their toil. For if they fall, one will lift up his fellow. But woe to him who is alone when he falls and has not another to lift him up!" (Ecclesiastes 4:9–10)

Holidays are the worst. It was Memorial Day weekend and my plans had changed due to an emergency in Clifford's family. My fellow Moody Bible Institute classmate, Mark, had graciously welcomed me into his home as I traveled the United States that first summer after Melodee's promotion.

It was in the mall, as Mark was looking for shirts for his upcoming business trip, that I felt the darkness coming. How does that happen? How does a seemingly routine errand begin to devolve into a discouraging situation? Surrounded by care and concern, having welcomed me into their hearts and home, how could I have begun to stumble down that Path of Gloom?

Later, over frozen yogurt, we began to talk of ministry, methods, and our alma mater. The gloom receded some and the light began to dawn afresh. It occurred to me as our conversation unfolded that in my current grief status, if I was not talking about ministry, I was struggling with the loneliness issue. I also realized that if I was not talking to a few of the people I care about the most, I was struggling with the loneliness issue. That was simply the reality of where I was, again, on this holiday.

Holidays Are Hard

Looking backwards, I could see a pattern. Easter was devastating. Melodee's birthday, April 30, was incredibly difficult. Mother's Day, the one holiday I thought I had a handle on, fell apart and had me calling my fellow grief traveler and hope giver, Gigi, at work the Monday afterwards.

Her wisdom was powerful and provided the North Star I needed on this Memorial Day to keep my nose pointed in the right direction and to not slip into the abyss that had claimed me on Easter. She had told me, "You will have a lot of these this year, each holiday to be exact. But you are growing stronger. They will get easier. Look how far you have already come. I'm proud of you. You're going to make it. It will be okay."

And that was what I was facing that Memorial Day afternoon in a strange mall in Michigan some 3,400 miles from home, accompanying my friend, Mark, on his quest to find some work shirts for his trip – I was in another holiday without Melodee.

Now, to be honest, Memorial Day weekend had never been my favorite during our marriage. Melodee somehow felt that the day was dedicated to some huge cleaning project. It was like the day was to be a day of remembering to clean the garage – her favorite project for the day!

And now, as I staggered through the racks of shirts on clearance looking for something both economical and that fit Mark's taste, I lamented not being able to clean one more garage with the Ivory Beauty.

Hope for the Holidays

The bad news is that holidays keep coming. The calendar is filled with them. Those little boxes that normally function as oases of recreation for the rest our soul's need now become black holes we must seek to avoid being sucked into. So, how do we resist the pull and remain intact when these celebrations of the seasons come upon us?

Stay in the moment. The greatest test we experience is the ability to stay with the people and the activity we are in right now. When people choose to invite us into their lives, honor them by *being* there. While it can be so easy to be distracted by the pain of our hearts, we have to be intentional about not drifting away in our emotions. That Memorial Day's BBQ was where I was to be that afternoon and I was determined to enjoy it.

Refuse to feel sorry. At the center of my holiday hurts was a simple reality – I felt sorry for myself. There between the rows of shirts I figured it out: I had begun to succumb to the, "Woe is me. I'm in pain," syndrome. There, in the store, I started to talk to myself. "Stop it. Yes, you don't have a wife anymore. Yes, you don't have a wife *yet*. Yes, this isn't a happy occasion for you. BUT God has given you these great friends who are trying to do all they can to make a bad situation more enjoyable for you. Honor them. Get back into the moment."

Appreciate the kindnesses. When I started to slip into the discouragement, I took my eyes off of the sacrifice of my friends and put the sorry of my heart as my first priority. In reality, I was saying to them (though they didn't know it), "Even though you have opened your home, fed me, taken me to Detroit *twice* for sightseeing and done more than the second-mile effort on short notice, I simply think my heart-ache is more important."

Such thinking is selfish, and I had to tell myself that. Yes, I'm human. Yes, I hurt. But healing comes when I choose to *be* human! So, there, during that afternoon, I consciously chose to appreciate their kindness and sacrifice by *thanking them* and engaging in conversation with them.

Engage with the festivities. Since it was the Memorial Day weekend, the traditional BBQ was on the evening agenda. Zach and Shelly, newly married son-in-love and daughter, had just come back from the Dominican Republic on the afternoon flight. They joined us for dinner. At that moment I could have chosen to let them enjoy each other and catch up without me – I was staying in their basement bedroom after all – or I could come in and be sociable. I chose the latter and God blessed in a wonderful evening of laughing and talking and encouraging my heart.

Choose to be happy. As I walked to my temporary bedroom that evening I came to one more realization. If I wanted to heal and become whole again, I would have to choose my mood. Being sullen and gloomy wasn't a choice God wanted for me. In fact, His prescription is *just* the opposite. He says, *"A joyful heart is good medicine, but a crushed spirit dries up the bones."* (Proverbs 17:22)

If I were to climb out of the darkness of my grief, which had once again swallowed me up like the tide, I would have to choose happy, to *do* happy, to *be* happy. It was then I concluded that either my moods would rule me or I would rule my moods. I chose to rule my moods. I chose to be happy, despite the pain. I chose to engage and be human. In the process, I laughed, talked and walked right out of the gloom and right into the light of God's love for my broken heart.

Holidays come. And they will continue to come. Accepting the kindnesses of family and friends, whether it is an invitation out to dinner, time to talk over coffee, help with a project or a multitude of other ways they reach out to us, the choice is always ours. Will we *choose* to be human and experience victory over our grief or will be choose to be a victim and languish in our grief?

What we choose will determine whether we heal or not. Choosing to engage and allow people to help us will bring about our healing at a far faster rate than sitting in the darkness and hoping it will go away. What will you choose today?

Taking Action

Consider: Choosing to engage and allow people to help us will bring about our healing at a far faster rate than sitting in the darkness and hoping it will go away.

Trust: *"A joyful heart is good medicine, but a crushed spirit dries up the bones."* (Proverbs 17:22)

Act: I choose to rule my moods. I choose to be happy, despite the pain. I choose to engage and be human.

Epilogue
Gaining Strength

Walking into Death's Shadow Valley

"He makes me lie down... He leads me... He restores... He leads me... Even though I walk through the valley of the shadow of death, I will fear no evil, for you are with me; your rod and your staff, they comfort me." (Psalm 23:2–4)

Grief is a journey. We just have to keep walking. And while these ideas in this book are meant to help you through the difficult early days, I'm glad to report that there are better days ahead.

When I started this project I thought I would write one book. It would've been larger, but I discovered that it would've been more difficult. Not more difficult for me, but more difficult for you.

You see, we are all at different stages in grief. Some of us are at the beginning. Some of us are in the middle. And some of us are walking out of Death's Shadow Valley into the glorious light of the table prepared before us in the presence of our enemy, the last enemy, Death.

Entering Death's Shadow Valley

This book has attempted to share with you my thoughts and journey through the early days of that first year alone. To be honest this is the most difficult part of the journey. It is so hard to transition from all that we have known and loved to being alone.

While others don't understand it, and some will tell us to get over it, the reality is we are simply lost inside of it. The darkness overwhelms, and sometimes it sneaks up and strangles the life out of us.

It is been my desire that this book would give you not only hope but help in the midst of those tough days, those brutal days, when you first walk this Valley seemingly all alone. Yet the reality is we are not alone! And as I have tried to show you, God is with us and wants us to heal.

I cannot tell you why God does this, why He takes us through such pain and suffering. I just know that at some point many of us will suffer this pain, this shredding of our soul. And for that I am truly sorry for you. All I can tell you is God is near so we have nothing to fear. I tell you that because it's been true in my journey.

I encourage you to read back through the certain chapters that meant a lot to you, or in the days ahead, the chapters that you couldn't relate to yet. For I have found that as I healed, some days I made 3 three steps forward and as my friend, Erwin Lutzer would say, other days I made two steps backward.

On those days when you're working your way backwards, the words that you read in this book that God was trying to tell you may not have applied. Now they may. So review and reconsider some of the things that you've read already.

Walking Through Death's Shadow Valley

As I've said in this book, this is a journey THROUGH Death's Shadow Valley. You're not to camp here or to build a house here. It seems like wherever I am in this journey, I will run across somebody who is either put down their tent pegs or build their house in the darkness and gloom.

Nothing could be farther from the heart of God. He longs for your healing. He longs for you to laugh again. He longs for you to have the joy of the Holy Spirit as your predominant characteristic because He is faithful and He is in your life right now.

Having walked out of the Valley, I can tell you that you must continue to walk *through* it. God's told me to share some more with you in another book. And when I do I want to provide more tools, more illustrations, and more help to get you *through* Death's Shadow Valley.

Until then, let me promise you that God is not done with you. God has not left you. And while I cannot tell you why He has done what He has done, I have learned three simple lessons in my journey…

Whatever God does is right. I do not have the capacity to know all the things that the universe holds and all the purposes within the mind of God. But I have walked with him now long enough and through some of the bloodiest chapters of my life I have discovered that on the other side, God had a reason. God has a purpose. And whether we discover those things and whether we enjoy those things will be wholly determined by our trust in Him.

78

Whenever God does it, it is right. God's timing often seems wrong. It's just the nature of the intersection between reality and spirituality – of the temporal and the eternal – when Jesus is King of our lives. When Melodee was promoted, she was so young at 59. We had planned so much more and were excited about what God wanted to do with us in the next decade. And then it all ended.

How was I to know then what I know now? How was I to know that God had a plan for my life that was bigger? A plan that was more audacious than I could've imagined? It was a plan that was linked to a prayer I have been praying for 20 years before Melodee stepped on to Heaven's shore.

However God does it, it is right. With my deep devotion to Melodee, it is surely true that it took the pain of wretched grief to point me in the direction that I went as I walked out of Death's Shadow Valley. As I will share in my next book, God prepares us for the next chapter of our lives by using the things that He does in this chapter of our lives. All I want to say now is that *however* God does it, it is right.

Walking Out of Death's Shadow Valley

And I want to assure you, for those of us who choose to trust God and stay very, very close to Him; we will walk *out of* Death's Shadow Valley. Depending on the mission for the rest of your life, your faith at this point in your life, and your willingness to obey him every step of the way, your future grows exponentially more incredible.

If you would've told me on November 12, 2017, all that I know today about what God was doing, how He was doing it, and what He was leading me into, I would've laughed right in your face. But God's future for me has been amazing. Melodee's blessing of my life and releasing me to accomplish all God has for me before I step on to Heaven's shore opened the doors to where I am now.

I have been able to walk out of Death's Shadow Valley because of my strong faith in Jesus Christ as my Rescuer and my intimate walk with Him every day of my life since I knelt in surrender to Him as King of my life and Rescuer of my soul. If you do not know Jesus Christ is the King of your life or you do not have an intimate relationship with Him, I beg of you to look in the appendices of this book. There are two tools that will be tremendously helpful.

I am encouraging you to read your Bible every day. If you have a copy you don't understand, get one in a more contemporary language that you do understand. And I am encouraging you to read the Bible with fresh eyes. When I started reading the Bible with fresh eyes, my whole world changed.

The resource, "How to Read the Bible With Fresh Eyes," will show you more of the "how to do" what I'm describing. But let me just say that when I am seeking God's direction for the five major problems in my life and the five big dreams that I still have, and God speaks to those ten things on a *daily* basis, I cannot but be changed for the better.

My problems and issues diminish and are resolved. My hopes and dreams have been realized time and again. And I attribute it all to the Word of God (the Bible) as it is applied to me by the Spirit of God (the Holy Spirit), because I have surrendered to King Jesus who is God. Your life will forever be different, better, healed, and joyful if you will do the same.

Thank you for being willing to walk with me through this journey of entering Death's Shadow Valley. To discover the next resource in this series, please sign up for notifications at Eaglesinleadership.org.

And now let me pray for you…

Lord God of compassion and comfort, while we do not understand why we are walking this dark and gloomy path, we want to say that we trust you; that we are surrendered to you. We echo the prayer of our King Jesus in the garden so long ago, "Not my will, but yours be done."

Bless each individual man or woman who is reading these words right now with life and strength and hope and healing. Give them the courage to take the steps necessary to walk, and keep walking, through The Valley of the Shadow of Death. Help them to fear no evil because You are with them. This is the message of Christmas, that the baby in the manger was Emmanuel, "God with us."

So I pray, that the child whom You sent to die for our sin, who was raised from the dead as King and Lord of life, might sustain and encourage and lead the person reading these words *through* and *out of* Death's Shadow Valley and into the new life of light and love that you have waiting for them. For the global glories of King Jesus, amen.

Taking Action

Consider: If you do not know Jesus Christ is the King of your life or you do not have an intimate relationship with Him, I beg of you to look in the appendices of this book.

Trust: *"He makes me lie down... He leads me... He restores... He leads me... Even though I walk through the valley of the shadow of death, I will fear no evil, for you are with me; your rod and your staff, they comfort me."* **(Psalm 23:2–4)**

Act: Read your Bible every day. If you have a copy you don't understand, get one in a more contemporary language that you do understand.

Appendix 1
How to Read the Bible with Fresh Eyes

The Process Is Simple!

"Draw near to God, and he will draw near to you." (James 4:8)

One of the best ways to heal from grief is to draw very close to God! A few years before Melodee's recurrence of cancer I discovered this incredible way to read God's Word, the Bible. I actually stumbled across the process through an everyday occurrence. I had lost my keys.

I can remember needing to get to an appointment at 1 p.m. But here I was 15 minutes before the appointment, and (as I drew painfully close to being late) I was tearing up the house trying to find my keys to the car and my office.

It was an amazing search, even if I do say so myself. I found things that had been lost for weeks. I even found some money! But nothing I found brought me any joy until I finally located my keys! And that's when I discovered how to read the Bible in a much better, more personal, and if I may say so a clearer way to hear God's voice speaking to my life.

"Reading the Bible with Fresh Eyes," is about using that methodology of searching for your keys, or whatever else you've lost, and applying it to reading the Bible. In the next steps, which are simple, you can find and hear God's answers to your biggest problems and His direction to your biggest dreams.

In the process I know that he will help you walk through the Valley of the Shadow of Death *and right on out of it!* So please, use this resource and enjoy hearing the voice of God as He works with the Spirit of God to lead you in the path that the Son of God has desired for your life from this day forward.

The process is simple:

1) **Get** a fresh Bible, preferably in a translation you haven't read before or for a while.
2) **Ask** God to open your eyes, your ears and your heart as He speaks to you through His Word each time you read.
3) **Read** the chapters on the included schedule each day out loud, slowly. (Appendix 2. Also available for free at *EaglesInLeadership.org*)

4) **Create** two (2) lists. One list is about the "5 Hopes and Dreams God Has Given to Me" and the other list is about the "5 Issues or Problems That I Need God's Wisdom Concerning *(Be sure to include the issue of money!)*

5) **Search** for what the Bible says on those ten (10) issues. (Here are some samples from Doc's 2020 lists with starting questions. *There is NO LIMIT on the questions you can ask on each item.*):

   a. **Issue or Problem: How God Gives Money** – How does one obtain it? What do I have to do to receive it? What do I do with it once I have it?

   b. **Issue or Problem: Greater Faith** – What does it look like? How do I get it? What will I do when I have it?

   c. **Issue or Problem: Prayer That Changes Things** – What kind of prayers does God listen and respond to? What kind of prayers does God ignore? How does my attitudes, actions, desperation, anxiety, and faith affect God answering my prayers?

   d. **Issue or Problem: Courage** – How does is come to me? How do I keep it? What does it look like? What will I do when I have it?

   e. **Hope or Dream: Expansion** – How does God expand my life? What parts of my life does God want to expand? What is the process I must go through when God starts to expand my life? What does God do to others when He expands my life?

   f. **Hope or Dream: Health** – How does God give health? What do I need to do to be healthy? Are there foods I should and shouldn't eat according to God? How do I live a long and healthy life? What else should I know in order to be healthy?

   g. **Hope or Dream: Sons** – To whom does God give sons? Why does He give them? What should I do to have sons? Once I have sons, what does God want me to do with them?

   h. **Hope or Dream: Visions** – To whom does God give visions? Why does He give them? Once He gives a vision, what should I do about it?

6) **Listen** to the whispers of the Spirit as you read, as He reveals God's will concerning your hopes and dreams and issues and problems.

7) **Write down** what you discover in a notebook or on a document file in your computer to review, ponder and pray about.

8) **Share** what you are learning with others in your church or small group and with family and friends to encourage them in the Lord.

Each time I read the Word of God, I am amazed at how practical His will and whim is. It encourages our souls, transforming us into His image each day we step into His presence through His Word.

~ Doc Smith

Kiwatule, Kampala, Uganda, January 2020

EaglesInLeadership.org

Appendix 2
Reading the Bible Cover to Cover Each Year
It's About 3 Chapters a Day!

"All Scripture is breathed out by God and profitable for teaching, for reproof, for correction, and for training in righteousness, that the man of God may be complete, equipped for every good work." (2 Timothy 3:16–17)

Since 1993 I have read the Bible cover to cover every year. Sometimes I have read it more than once. From those earliest days I developed a simple reading schedule that is designed to read the Bible the way it was written… from the front to the back, like every other book I've read.

When I did this the first time, with my dear friend and deacon Roberto to encourage me, we found God changing us in amazing and real ways. Now, for over two decades, I have watched the same thing happen to people from all over the world as they, too, read God's Word on a daily basis cover to cover.

Here are some tips for reading through the Bible:

- **READ…** The passage for the day, listening closely for what God is saying.
- **EXPLORE…** what the Bible has to say by asking questions.
- **ACT…** on the truth by finding one thing to DO.
- **PRAY…** the verses you have just read back to God.

Below is the simple plan. Enjoy it!

January

In the Beginning

Jan-1	**Genesis** 1-3	Jan-9	**Genesis** 25-27
Jan-2	**Genesis** 4-6	Jan-10	**Genesis** 28-30
Jan-3	**Genesis** 7-9	Jan-11	**Genesis** 31-33
Jan-4	**Genesis** 10-12	Jan-12	**Genesis** 34-36
Jan-5	**Genesis** 13-15	Jan-13	**Genesis** 37-39
Jan-6	**Genesis** 16-18	Jan-14	**Genesis** 40-42
Jan-7	**Genesis** 19-21	Jan-15	**Genesis** 43-45
Jan-8	**Genesis** 22-24	Jan-16	**Genesis** 46-48

Mar-17   **Joshua** 11-13
Mar-18   **Joshua** 14-16
Mar-19   **Joshua** 17-19
Mar-20   **Joshua** 20-21
Mar-21   **Joshua** 22-24
Mar-22   **Judges** 1-2
Mar-23   **Judges** 3-5
Mar-24   **Judges** 6-7
Mar-25   **Judges** 8-9
Mar-26   **Judges** 10-11
Mar-27   **Judges** 12-14
Mar-28   **Judges** 15-17
Mar-29   **Judges** 18-19
Mar-30   **Judges** 20-21
Mar-31   **Ruth** 1-4

April

From Samuel to David

Apr-1   **I Samuel** 1-3
Apr-2   **I Samuel** 4-7
Apr-3   **I Samuel** 8-11
Apr-4   **I Samuel** 12-14:23
Apr-5   **I Samuel** 14:24-16
Apr-6   **I Samuel** 17-18
Apr-7   **I Samuel** 19-21
Apr-8   **I Samuel** 22-24
Apr-9   **I Samuel** 25-27
Apr-10   **I Samuel** 28-31
Apr-11   **II Samuel** 1-2
Apr-12   **II Samuel** 3-5
Apr-13   **II Samuel** 6-9
Apr-14   **II Samuel** 10-12
Apr-15   **II Samuel** 13-14
Apr-16   **II Samuel** 15-16
Apr-17   **II Samuel** 17-18

Apr-18   **II Samuel** 19-20
Apr-19   **II Samuel** 21-22
Apr-20   **II Samuel** 23-24

From Solomon to exile

Apr-21   **I Kings** 1-2:25
Apr-22   **I Kings** 2:26-4
Apr-23   **I Kings** 5-7
Apr-24   **I Kings** 8
Apr-25   **I Kings** 9-11
Apr-26   **I Kings** 12-13
Apr-27   **I Kings** 14-15
Apr-28   **I Kings** 16-18
Apr-29   **I Kings** 19-20
Apr-30   **I Kings** 21-22

May

May-1   **II Kings** 1-3
May-2   **II Kings** 4-5
May-3   **II Kings** 6-8
May-4   **II Kings** 9-10
May-5   **II Kings** 11-13
May-6   **II Kings** 14-15
May-7   **II Kings** 16-17
May-8   **II Kings** 18-20
May-9   **II Kings** 21-23
May-10   **II Kings** 24-25

From David to exile

May-11   **I Chronicles** 1-2
May-12   **I Chronicles** 3-5
May-13   **I Chronicles** 6-7
May-14   **I Chronicles** 8-10
May-15   **I Chronicles** 11-13
May-16   **I Chronicles** 14-16

May-17   **I Chronicles** 17-20
May-18   **I Chronicles** 21-23
May-19   **I Chronicles** 24-26
May-20   **I Chronicles** 27-29
May-21   **II Chronicles** 1-3
May-22   **II Chronicles** 4-6
May-23   **II Chronicles** 7-9
May-24   **II Chronicles** 10-13
May-25   **II Chronicles** 14-17
May-26   **II Chronicles** 18-20
May-27   **II Chronicles** 21-24
May-28   **II Chronicles** 25-27
May-29   **II Chronicles** 28-30
May-30   **II Chronicles** 31-33
May-31   **II Chronicles** 34-36

June

Times of restoration
Jun-1   **Ezra** 1-2
Jun-2   **Ezra** 3-5
Jun-3   **Ezra** 6-7
Jun-4   **Ezra** 8-9
Jun-5   **Ezra** 10
Jun-6   **Nehemiah** 1-3
Jun-7   **Nehemiah** 4-6
Jun-8   **Nehemiah** 7-8
Jun-9   **Nehemiah** 9-10
Jun-10   **Nehemiah** 11-12
Jun-11   **Nehemiah** 13
Jun-12   **Esther** 1-3
Jun-13   **Esther** 4-7
Jun-14   **Esther** 8-10

God's faithful servant
Jun-15   **Job** 1-4

Jun-16   **Job** 5-8
Jun-17   **Job** 9-12
Jun-18   **Job** 13-16
Jun-19   **Job** 17-20
Jun-20   **Job** 21-24
Jun-21   **Job** 25-29
Jun-22   **Job** 30-33
Jun-23   **Job** 34-37
Jun-24   **Job** 38-40
Jun-25   **Job** 41-42

Songs of praise
Jun-26   **Psalms** 1-9
Jun-27   **Psalms** 10-17
Jun-28   **Psalms** 18-22
Jun-29   **Psalms** 23-30
Jun-30   **Psalms** 31-35

July

Jul-1   **Psalms** 36-39
Jul-2   **Psalms** 40-45
Jul-3   **Psalms** 46-51
Jul-4   **Psalms** 52-59
Jul-5   **Psalms** 60-66
Jul-6   **Psalms** 67-71
Jul-7   **Psalms** 72-77
Jul-8   **Psalms** 78-80
Jul-9   **Psalms** 81-87
Jul-10   **Psalms** 88-91
Jul-11   **Psalms** 92-100
Jul-12   **Psalms** 101-105
Jul-13   **Psalms** 106-107
Jul-14   **Psalms** 108-118
Jul-15   **Psalm** 119
Jul-16   **Psalms** 120-131

Jul-17   **Psalms** 132-138
Jul-18   **Psalms** 139-143
Jul-19   **Psalms** 144-150

Wisdom for life
Jul-20   **Proverbs** 1-3
Jul-21   **Proverbs** 4-7
Jul-22   **Proverbs** 8-11
Jul-23   **Proverbs** 12-15
Jul-24   **Proverbs** 16-19
Jul-25   **Proverbs** 20-22
Jul-26   **Proverbs** 23-26
Jul-27   **Proverbs** 27-31
Jul-28   **Ecclesiastes** 1-4
Jul-29   **Ecclesiastes** 5-8
Jul-30   **Ecclesiastes** 9-12
Jul-31   **Song of Sol.** 1-8

August

Hope for God's people
Aug-1   **Isaiah** 1-4
Aug-2   **Isaiah** 5-9
Aug-3   **Isaiah** 10-14
Aug-4   **Isaiah** 15-21
Aug-5   **Isaiah** 22-26
Aug-6   **Isaiah** 27-31
Aug-7   **Isaiah** 32-37
Aug-8   **Isaiah** 38-42
Aug-9   **Isaiah** 43-46
Aug-10   **Isaiah** 47-51
Aug-11   **Isaiah** 52-57
Aug-12   **Isaiah** 58-63
Aug-13   **Isaiah** 64-66

Tears for God's people

Aug-14   **Jeremiah** 1-3
Aug-15   **Jeremiah** 4-6
Aug-16   **Jeremiah** 7-10
Aug-17   **Jeremiah** 11-14
Aug-18   **Jeremiah** 15-18
Aug-19   **Jeremiah** 19-22
Aug-20   **Jeremiah** 23-25
Aug-21   **Jeremiah** 26-28
Aug-22   **Jeremiah** 29-31
Aug-23   **Jeremiah** 32-33
Aug-24   **Jeremiah** 34-36
Aug-25   **Jeremiah** 37-40
Aug-26   **Jeremiah** 41-44
Aug-27   **Jeremiah** 45-48
Aug-28   **Jeremiah** 49-50
Aug-29   **Jeremiah** 51-52
Aug-30   **Lament.** 1-2
Aug-31   **Lament.** 3-5

September

Something new
Sep-1   **Ezekiel** 1-4
Sep-2   **Ezekiel** 5-9
Sep-3   **Ezekiel** 10-13
Sep-4   **Ezekiel** 14-16
Sep-5   **Ezekiel** 17-19
Sep-6   **Ezekiel** 20-21
Sep-7   **Ezekiel** 22-24
Sep-8   **Ezekiel** 25-28
Sep-9   **Ezekiel** 29-32
Sep-10   **Ezekiel** 33-36
Sep-11   **Ezekiel** 37-39
Sep-12   **Ezekiel** 40-42
Sep-13   **Ezekiel** 43-45
Sep-14   **Ezekiel** 46-48

Lions & visions

Sep-15 **Daniel** 1-3
Sep-16 **Daniel** 4-6
Sep-17 **Daniel** 7-9
Sep-18 **Daniel** 10-12

The minor prophets

Sep-19 **Hosea** 1-6
Sep-20 **Hosea** 7-14
Sep-21 **Joel** 1-3
Sep-22 **Amos** 1-5
Sep-23 **Amos** 6-**Obadiah** 1
Sep-24 **Jonah** 1-4
Sep-25 **Micah** 1-7
Sep-26 **Nahum** 1-**Hab**. 3
Sep-27 **Zephaniah** 1-**Haggai** 2
Sep-28 **Zechariah** 1-7
Sep-29 **Zechariah** 8-14
Sep-30 **Malachi** 1-4

October

The good news!

Oct-1 **Matthew** 1-4
Oct-2 **Matthew** 5-6
Oct-3 **Matthew** 7-9
Oct-4 **Matthew** 10-11
Oct-5 **Matthew** 12
Oct-6 **Matthew** 13-14
Oct-7 **Matthew** 15-17
Oct-8 **Matthew** 18-20
Oct-9 **Matthew** 21-22
Oct-10 **Matthew** 23-24
Oct-11 **Matthew** 25-26
Oct-12 **Matthew** 27-28

The story of Jesus

Oct-13 **Mark** 1-3
Oct-14 **Mark** 4-5
Oct-15 **Mark** 6-7
Oct-16 **Mark** 8-9
Oct-17 **Mark** 10-11
Oct-18 **Mark** 12-13
Oct-19 **Mark** 14-16

Joy to the world

Oct-20 **Luke** 1
Oct-21 **Luke** 2-3
Oct-22 **Luke** 4-5
Oct-23 **Luke** 6-7
Oct-24 **Luke** 8-9
Oct-25 **Luke** 10-11
Oct-26 **Luke** 12-13
Oct-27 **Luke** 14-16
Oct-28 **Luke** 17-18
Oct-29 **Luke** 19-20
Oct-30 **Luke** 21-22
Oct-31 **Luke** 23-24

November

Light for the world

Nov-1 **John** 1-3
Nov-2 **John** 4-5
Nov-3 **John** 6-8
Nov-4 **John** 9-10
Nov-5 **John** 11-12
Nov-6 **John** 13-16
Nov-7 **John** 17-18
Nov-8 **John** 19-21

The new church

Nov-9   **Acts** 1-3

Nov-10   **Acts** 4-6

Nov-11   **Acts** 7-8

Nov-12   **Acts** 9-10

Nov-13   **Acts** 11-13

Nov-14   **Acts** 14-16

Nov-15   **Acts** 17-19

Nov-16   **Acts** 20-22

Nov-17   **Acts** 23-25

Nov-18   **Acts** 26-28

We live by faith

Nov-19   **Romans** 1-3

Nov-20   **Romans** 4-7

Nov-21   **Romans** 8-10

Nov-22   **Romans** 11-13

Nov-23   **Romans** 14-16

Nov-24   **I Corinthians** 1-4

Nov-25   **I Corinthians** 5-9

Nov-26   **I Corinthians** 10-13

Nov-27   **I Corinthians** 14-16

Nov-28   **II Corinthians** 1-4

Nov-29   **II Corinthians** 5-8

Nov-30   **II Corinthians** 9-13

December

How to live for Jesus

Dec-1   **Galatians** 1-3

Dec-2   **Galatians** 4-6

Dec-3   **Ephesians** 1-3

Dec-4   **Ephesians** 4-6

Dec-5   **Philippians** 1-4

Dec-6   **Colossians** 1-4

Dec-7   **I Thessalonians** 1-5

Dec-8   **II Thessalonians** 1-3

Dec-9   **I Timothy** 1-6

Dec-10   **II Timothy** 1-4

Dec-11   **Titus** 1 – **Philemon** 1

Jesus finished God's plan

Dec-12   **Hebrews** 1-4

Dec-13   **Hebrews** 5-7

Dec-14   **Hebrews** 8-10

Dec-15   **Hebrews** 11-13

Dec-16   **James** 1-5

Dec-17   **I Peter** 1-2

Dec-18   **I Peter** 3-5

Dec-19   **II Peter** 1-3

Dec-20   **I John** 1-3

Dec-21   **I John** 4-5

Dec-22   **II John** 1 – **Jude** 1

A vision for the church

Dec-23   **Revelation** 1-2

Dec-24   **Revelation** 3-5

Dec-25   **Revelation** 6-8

Dec-26   **Revelation** 9-11

Dec-27   **Revelation** 12-13

Dec-28   **Revelation** 14-16

Dec-29   **Revelation** 17-18

Dec-30   **Revelation** 19-20

Dec-31   **Revelation** 21-22

Congratulations! You have finished one of the greatest accomplishments that any believer in Christ can strive for: reading through the Bible in one year!

The Intimacy with God Series

God created you to love you!

In His Image is the next step for those who have read The Purpose Driven Life. Following the Life Purpose of Mission, this book explores God's great love for humanity from every book of the Bible.

God welcomes you into His presence with joy and pleasure!

In His Presence is a daily devotional which targets the purpose of Magnification (Worship). It revolves around the Biblical truth, "God welcomes you into His presence with joy and pleasure." The devotional follows a reading schedule through the entire book of Psalms over the course of the year.

In each daily devotional...

• There is a Biblical Scripture they are encouraged to read;

• There is a passage of Scripture to read in the devotional itself;

• There is the devotional to read which focuses the reader on a single thought, broken into two, three or four practical ideas they can utilize that day in their lives; and

• There is a thought to take with the reader each day that summarizes the theme concerning God's great love for them.

**Available Now at
EaglesinLeadership.org**

Want to Get the Most Out of Your Daily Devotions?

The Word in Worship Daily Devotional Journal. This powerful tool allows you to step into the very presence of God in such a way that you begin to understand the heart of God. This journal features two major sections:

Bible Highlights Reading Log. This journal allows you to answer 4 key questions based on 2 Timothy 3.16-17. With each day, your responses to these probes into the Word of God reveal the passion and compassion, the path and power of God! Each journal includes a special prayer which asks God to open His Word using Biblical texts. A reading schedule is also included.

Personal Prayer Journal. No one can pray for everything every day! Breaking our prayer lives into a manageable manner is the result of this prayer journal. Each day we pray for the urgent things in our lives. Then, organizing our prayer needs into a daily log allows us to intercede for things like personal and family needs, friends both inside and outside the church, church leaders, missionaries and political leaders. Each journal provides an intimate prayer which allows us to adore God and confess our failures before we proceed into His presence.

Available Now at EaglesinLeadership.org

The Living in Christ Series

Hope Enabler
by Mrs. Melodee Joy Smith

Finding hope in troubling times can be hard. Relying solely on God to sustain you may seem impossible, but help is always on the way, and that's the focus of Melodee Smith's book, *Hope Enabler*.

About Melodee Smith

Melodee Joy Smith is a pastor's wife ministering in Southern California. Alongside her husband, Dr. Matthew Lee Smith she's counseled families, spoke at conferences and trained Christian leaders.

Want Dr. Matthew Lee Smith to Speak at Your Event, Church or Conference?

Servant leadership in today's world is much different from business leadership. Doc speaks on a variety of topics that touch today's world.

- **Leading With Significance**

- **Teamwork in Turbulent Times**

- **Soaring With Eagles In Leadership**

- **VIP Treatment In A Self-Service World**

- **Created To Be Creative**

- **Urbanology 101 - Building a Lasting Church in an Urban Environment**

- **Building People Able to Reach Their Community For Christ!**

- **Help! Our Community Is Changing!**

- **How To Have An Exciting Daily Devotional!**

Plus many, many more! You can schedule Doc to speak to your group, event or organization by contacting him at Events@EaglesInLeadership.org

About the Author

Dr. Matthew Lee Smith is an author, speaker, pastor and professor. His heart's mission is to "Encourage Achievement in Godly Leaders by Emphasizing Servanthood (EAGLES)." He mentors and encourages men and women of God to realize God's purpose for their lives as revealed through His word. Currently living in Los Angeles, California with his wife, Kate Akello, Dr. Smith enjoys a passionate relationship with God, reading the Bible at least once per year and garnering hundreds of new insights monthly from God's Word. For more information about the author please visit him at EaglesInLeadership.org.

The Reaching Our World Series

Growing Missional Leaders is a practical, passionate, Biblical mentoring journey for individuals, small groups, leadership teams and congregations who desire to win their world for Christ.

Readers will appreciate the enthusiastic and Spirit-filled hope God provides as Doc ...

• Tells stories – of lost opportunities and successes with friends that give powerful encouragement of personal and corporate   outreach.

• Opens Bible passages – again and again – showing God's heart is to bring his lost children home.

• Provides stimulating discussion questions – at the end of each chapter – providing the stepping-stones to launching fresh ministry into your community.

Believers hungering to reach their world for Christ will be energized by this passionate call to fulfill Christ's Gospel and the invigorating manner in which their thought processes will be s-t-r-e-t-c-h-e-d to God-sized proportions.

The Reaching Our World Series

Gathering Missional Leaders continues this series with more practical, passionate, Biblical mentoring for individuals, small groups, leadership teams and congregations who desire to create an environment for exponential leadership development.

Gathering Missional Leaders ...

- Explores the elements necessary to build the habitat that will attract a strong and vibrant coalition of men and women who want to reach their world in their generation!

- Is set up as a guided study. Whether you study alone, with someone, with your small group, leadership team or entire congregation, you will appreciate the discussion questions after each chapter.

- Is designed to stir your soul and allow you to hear the Spirit of God's heart and desire for your life.

Ministry Resources from Eagles in Leadership

Free Resources:

Transformed! is an award-winning weekly audio podcast from Eagles in Leadership. Each week you can download or listen to Dr. Matthew Lee Smith

as he encourages the people of God. Transformed! also features interviews with great Christian leaders such as Zig Zigler, Jentezen Franklin, Alex Kendrick and Max Lucado as well as great interviews with Christian recording artists such as Matthew West.

This free resource is available at EaglesInLeadership.org

The Eagles in Leadership blog is designed to enhance your God-given "eagle" qualities in leadership. It is our sincere hope you will find these posts helpful and s-t-r-e-t-c-h-i-n-g

in their content and will provide the steps you need to take to "soar with the eagles" in every aspect of your personal, spiritual, family, career and ministry life!

Subscribe to this free resource at EaglesInLeadership.org

Israel and Beyond Faith Tours

Yes! Walk Where Jesus Walked!

- Breathe in the fresh air of the Galilee!
- Relive the Sermon on the Mount WHERE it was delivered by Jesus!
- Listen to Peter make his confession of Jesus as the Messiah at Caesarea Phillipi (Banias)!
- Envision the epic battle between Elijah and the prophets of Baal at Mount Carmel (Muchraka)!
- Be baptized where John led so many into repentance on the Jordan River at Yardenit, our Baptismal Site!
- Prepare for Christmas in Bethlehem at the Church of Nativity and Shepherds' Field!
- Come up to Jerusalem, the Capitol City of God on Planet Earth!
- Walk through the Old City of David and take in the sights, sounds, and smells of Jerusalem!
- See where Jesus was tortured on the Gabbatha pavement inside the Roman Stronghold!
- Pray at The Western Wall and ask God to fulfill His promise to YOU through King Solomon's prayer of dedicating the 1st Temple in 1 Kings 8!
- Reverently walkthrough Masada where the last stand of the Jewish Zealots against the oppressive rule of the Romans met a tragic end and a glorious rallying cry for today's Israel: "Never again!"

- Float in the rejuvenating waters of the Dead Sea, the lowest point on earth!
- Discover Qumran, where the Dead Sea Scrolls were discovered in 1947!
- Splash in the waters of Ein Gedi where King David sheltered from the wrath of King Saul!
- Pray in the Mount of Olives as Jesus often did and witness the outstanding view of Jerusalem!
- Stand in the Room of the Last Supper on Mount Zion where Jesus spent his last free hours together with those He loved the most!
- Fall to your knees in the Garden of Gethsemane and utter the words of Jesus there in total surrender to your crucified King ... "Not my will but YOURS be done!"
- Walk quietly into the Garden Tomb and see Golgotha (Calvary) before having a memorable Communion service!
- And SO MUCH MORE!

Join Dr. Matthew and Kate Smith in Israel for a truly life-changing, once in a lifetime event!

Details are just a CLICK away on the link below!

**Available Now at
EaglesinLeadership.org/tour**

www.ingramcontent.com/pod-product-compliance
Lightning Source LLC
Chambersburg PA
CBHW051430150726
48000CB00005B/2037